VERY FEW ROSES – EVEN LESS HONEY!

Very Few Roses – Even Less Honey!

One Man's Life

by

Jack Oliver Davis

Founder of Hospital Metalcraft Ltd (Bristol Maid Hospital Equipment) in 1953 and Managing Director and Chairman until retirement in 2002.

Not quite a story of rags to riches – but possibly from nothing to adequacy, and a lasting satisfaction of having contributed to the success of the company.

The descriptions of events, incidents and characters featured in this book
are true and correct according to the recollections of the author

© Jack Oliver Davis 2002

First published in 2002 on behalf of the author
by Scotforth Books,
Carnegie House,
Chatsworth Road,
Lancaster LA1 4SL,
England
Tel: +44(0)1524 840111
Fax: +44(0)1524 840222
email: carnegie@provider.co.uk
Publishing and book sales: www.carnegiepub.co.uk
Book production: www.wooof.net

British Library Cataloguing-in-Publication data
A catalogue record for this book is available from the British Library

ISBN 1-904244-20-8

Typeset by George Wishart & Associates, Whitley Bay
Printed and bound in the UK by
The Cromwell Press, Wiltshire

Contents

Dedication

Dedicated to the two 'Glads' in my life, loving,
loyal wife, mother and grandmother and a
wonderful sister, mother and grandmother –
both entirely devoted to their families.

One Man's Life – Warts and All – of Jack Oliver Davis

Born 11th January, 1918 in a gamekeeper's 'house', a corrugated iron bungalow set in a small clearing in woodlands near Old Alresford, Hampshire, to Amy Beatrice and Charles Davis – at last a brother for 6 sisters – the eldest Adeline (Addy), Amy (Ame), Hilda (Hilly), Eva (Eve), Nora (Nore), Gladys (Glad – Gladdy when I wanted to annoy her!).

As mother had just received a letter from my soldier father serving in Palestine on the Mount of Olives there was probably no hesitation in naming me – although I have always been grateful that it was chosen as my middle name!

My first recollection of my father was when I was nearly 4 years old – a very big upright figure of a man – then a gamekeeper and rarely seen without a gun on his shoulder. Shortly afterwards he moved to start his own business as a smallholder, but not before my very first memory of breaking icicles reaching down from the roof and putting them on the path to make the foxes, always around after dark, slip up!

Father had bought a small wooden pre-fabricated bungalow with felted roof and erected it temporarily in a rented field whilst waiting to take possession of a much larger field a few miles away. A few chickens, ducks, goats and two horses – a skittish mare called Peggy and a light cart horse, Peter.

I have a distinct memory of getting into trouble when I was about 4½ years old – Eve was learning to ride Addys' bike on the road outside the bungalow – I was upset and jealous

1

because she wouldn't give me a ride, so I threw a stick over the hedge which caught in a wheel causing her to fall off. Following a short chase, I received a good slapping!! One morning we were wakened by father and told both horses were missing and we were all sent out to look for them. Peter was quickly found – as was a gap in the hedge which hadn't been there the previous day. No sign of Peggy – whereupon father jumped on Addy's bike telling mother not to worry and us to repair the gap. He returned some hours later leading Peggy, accompanied by the local policeman who had gone with father to a gypsy camp some 5 miles away where he found Peggy 'being looked after', having been found straying! A likely story!

When I was 5, I was sent to the village school at Grately, some 2 miles away, chaperoned by Nore and Glad – where I was involved in a nasty accident a few days later. At midday lunch break we were all gathered round the iron combustion stove in the middle of the room, mostly sitting on the floor but a few – including myself – sitting on top of the iron fireguard. Suddenly the other children jumped off – I overbalanced and crashed to the floor – and the half round top rail of the fireguard cut off the finger of a boy sitting on the floor with hand outstretched.

I later told mother that he had 'rice' coming out of his finger and asked her if all our fingers were filled with rice! (Many years later I was to learn that the finger had been 'crushed' off and not cut off – the 'rice' being the bloodless mangled flesh and bone left on the stump of the finger!)

A few weeks later father took possession of his new field at Middlecot, near Quarley and we moved into a real house with stairs for a few weeks whilst father moved and re-erected the bungalow on the side of a hill fronting the field. The back of

Father and Mother, 1940.

the bungalow was at ground level, the front built up some 4 feet above ground level leaving open space below, much to my dismay later, as our free range chicken used to nest at the back beneath the bungalow and it became one of my weekly jobs to crawl into this space – only 6" or 7" high at the back – and recover the eggs. Leaving me with a feeling of claustrophobia which has remained ever since!

The bungalow was about 20 feet long and 18 feet front to back with a 3 foot wide central passage front to back with a door to the outside at each end, not that we could ever use these doors, as father built wooden 'beds' at each end with blankets screening each 'bedroom' so formed with 4 rooms, 2 each side of the passage, one being my elder sisters' bedroom, one mother and father's, one the 'sitting room' and the other the living room. This had a long table on one side, with bench seats on either side, the table always being covered with shiny patterned oilcloth. Cupboards holding food, crockery etc. took up the rest of the space. Father cut a 'door' in the end of the room leading to a quite large (at least it seemed large to me!) leanto with corrugated iron walls and roof – and a door leading to outside. This was mum's kitchen – housing a big iron range with ovens on each side of the open fire – where there was always a very big black kettle, this being the source of all hot water and cooking. Outside the back door was a large water butt collecting water from the roof – used for all purposes except drinking and cooking. The range was wood fired – it being Glad's and my job to make sure there was always plenty of wood cut ready for use!

A smaller kettle with drinking water was also always on the range – again it being one of our jobs to keep another water butt topped up from a fresh water standpipe about 150 yards away near the closest of the chicken houses. The 'kitchen' floor was of packed earth – covered with several layers of lino. Father had dug a further flattened area outside the back door into the hillside – again with packed earth floor, corrugated iron roof and part walling containing a long galvanized tin bath – this was the washroom and bathroom for all the family – not a lot of privacy for anyone!

There was no electricity or gas – a large oil lamp susp-ended from the roof above the living room table provided the only illumination, supplemented by candles in the kitchen and wash room, if the wind wasn't too strong! The partition walls were only about 6ft high, so enough light percolated over the top to enable us to go to bed and dress in the dark mornings – no candles allowed as these were for adults only!

On the long dark evenings, once we had finished our chores for the day, chickens locked away and supper over, a brief time was allowed for reading under the hanging oil lamp and we were packed off to bed. No light allowed of course and so Glad and I invented a game of 'I spy with my little eye' after promising 'God's Promise' not to change the object once chosen ('S' for skewer could not be changed to saucepan if correctly called first time) Each object had to be able to be seen in daylight within or near to home – 'L' for lavatory or 'T' for tap were not permissible as both were too far away.

Tiring of this we would have a round of spelling, later turning to mental arithmetic, hence we became quite good at both.

Eventually Mother and Father would call out telling us to stop talking and go to sleep, but not before we had one last game – who could make the longest 'goodnight' – stretching out each word whilst the other counted the seconds. I almost always lost, accusing Glad next morning of counting the seconds too slowly when she timed me!

We attended the village school at Quarley about an hour's walk away providing you knew all the short cuts across fields, through woods. Father had quickly built up a regular clientele with various army units – officers, NCOs, other ranks, messes at nearby Tidworth, Larkhill army camps etc. supplying dressed chicken, eggs and rabbits – with deliveries on Saturdays. This meant we children and mother spending many hours after school on Fridays, plus early Saturday mornings preparing the produce.

Father put all the chickens to be killed, anything from 150 to 500, off into a shed, and it was my job from the age of about

6 onwards to catch a chicken, wring its neck, pluck the breast feathers whilst still warm so as not to tear the flesh, and then hand it to one of my sisters to complete plucking, soon establishing a routine so that one of my sisters was ready to take over as soon as I finished plucking the breasts. Once the chicken was plucked, it was given to mother who gutted it, cut off legs and head and trussed it with a couple of wooden skewers and cotton twine (string). She was amazingly fast and frequently had to wait for the next chicken!

I well remember one hilarious (at least to us) occasion, when Glad had finished plucking a chicken and placed it on Mother's table only for it to 'come-to' and race out of the door causing me to chase this naked chicken and despatch it properly when caught. Needless to say I was never allowed to forget that mishap!

About 900–1,000 chicken were held in stock, this meant that father had to go to Salisbury and Andover markets every week to replenish stocks, by horse and cart at first, by Ford later on. Father always ensured that he was able to bring back all chickens bought at Salisbury market on Tuesdays but was rarely able to do likewise with any purchases at Andover on Fridays and would hand those crates of chicken he couldn't manage to the local carrier – a primitive bus carrying 10–12 passengers, with roof rack and a large 'open top crate' built on the back – holding goods purchased by passengers, our chickens and other goods sent by shops for delivery to villagers en route.

This carrier only went within about 1½ miles of our home and Nor, Glad and I were instructed to meet it at the nearest point – a place called Toplas Hill (so named, we were told, because a policeman of that name had been murdered there some years previously – certainly there were some stones marking the spot!) Dependant on the number of crates we sometimes had to make 2 or 3 trips to collect them all plus anything else father had bought. The carrier used to come past the school at Quarley, although some 2–2½ hours after school had closed. My sisters always went straight home from school, but I used to sneak off and wait for the carrier to come past then I ran out and hung onto the crate, having to drop off and hide every time the carrier stopped, getting a 'free' ride in all weathers for some 4½ miles. On one very wet day one of the passengers saw me drop off and knowing I was Charles Davis' son told the driver who agreed to let me ride in the cage at the back when father had crates of chicken for delivery. I think this was really because I could hand down items from the roof rack and cage when required – usually rolls of lino, furniture etc. to save him having to climb up every time! On one occasion there were no crates for us, the carrier didn't stop at Toplas Hill and I had to jump off the bus going at about 30 mph downhill, badly grazing my knees and arms – but little sympathy from my sisters!

My sisters and I all had regular jobs to do before and after school, let chickens out in the morning, get them all shut up at night, spread feed, water etc. for chickens, goats and about 40 Chinchilla rabbits kept for their pelts – these were housed in large mesh floored hutches which had to be moved weekly – plus collecting eggs and the usual chicken plucking on Fridays. Mother made special clothes for us to wear when doing the latter job – very necessary as we became infested with fleas – having to undress and bath outside on the bank before putting our normal clothes back on, leaving mother with the unpleasant task of boiling and washing our 'chicken clothes'!

Our one treat every year was a visit to Tidworth Military Tattoo. On one such occasion father was given two wire haired

The Davis Bungalow by the mid-1980s – hardly recognisable.

terrier puppies which we promptly named 'Tat' and 'Too'. Tat unfortunately died quite young but Tooey became a great pet and a very good rabbiter, going everywhere with Glad and myself unless Father was around with a gun on his shoulder – when we had to take a back seat!

On warm sunny evenings father and myself used to take Tooey out to adjacent fields, me and Tooey 'raising' rabbits lying out in hides for father to shoot, Dad being a very good shot as becomes a gamekeeper and rarely wasting a shot. On one such occasion we 'raised' three rabbits at the same time – father shot 2 (with his double barrelled gun) and Tooey carried on chasing the other one into a thorn thicket. We heard a yelp and on catching up with Tooey found he had a long thorn right in the centre of his eye. Father was very professional in this kind of circumstance and cut off the thorn leaving a short length – before taking him to the vet who confirmed there was nothing that could be done except leave the thorn after cutting it off as close as possible. Sure enough, within a few days he was back to normal and lived for a further 12 years or so when on one of his daily walks with my then invalid father, he failed to return home. I and some pals went searching for him, and found him lying in a hedge badly injured having been knocked down by a car. We carried him home where father shot him and we buried Tooey at the bottom of the garden.

One of our Saturday jobs was to peg out and salt rabbit skins – including those of our Chinchillas. Although I used to kill thousands of chicken and wild rabbits I could never bring myself to kill or eat the chinchillas! It was as much as I could do to peg out their pelts! These dried pelts used to be collected every 3–4 weeks by a Jewish dealer who paid 1d or 2d for wild rabbit skins, 5d or 6d for Chinchillas plus 4d or so for any mole skins we had managed to catch. Glad and I got into trouble with mother once when she was entertaining the Jewish gentleman to tea in our 'sitting room' and we heard him say, 'I tink this is nanny goat's milk – am I right?' whereupon we burst into loud laughter!

A regular Saturday afternoon job was to cut down trees – dead or live – in one of three plantations near our field, drag them home and saw them into lengths to fit the range, our only source of heating apart from the rarely used Primus stove.

I remember when I was about seven or eight years old there was very little time for playing, really only during the light evenings after we had finished our chores, and weekends, mostly climbing trees, making tree houses and dens – plus teasing our sisters and daring them to catch us!

Father once brought home a couple of bicycle wheels for us

to make a cart with, there was no wood around so we visited the village rubbish dump after school one day and found an old bicycle frame with wheels and front forks – but no handlebars! It was a man's frame and we managed to wire two heavy bolts in position to act as wheel axles and then cut a V shaped hawthorn branch and jammed it in position in top of the forks and we had a bike! No pedals, of course, but we spent hours taking it up to the top of the hill behind our house and careering down – totally out of control! Needless to say mother also spent hours treating our cuts and bruises and repairing our clothes! She had one infallible treatment for our cuts – really hot bread poultices which always seemed to work. She was not one to waste food, however and I later wondered if this was why we had so many bread puddings – still a great favourite of mine!

We all had tremendous respect, love and admiration for our parents. Always Mother and Father – never Mum or Dad – and we never ever saw or heard them rowing or arguing, although they must have done so, but never in our presence or hearing. Mother, despite having had 7–8 children, was very good looking and father although rather more remote, was always very approachable and certainly we could never remember either of them ever raising a hand to us although we certainly gave them enough reason to do so. A few sharp words were always enough to bring us to heel! Mother was plagued all her life by a very bad ulcerated leg although it never prevented her from working 15–16 hours a day – and the smell of Germolene was always with us. She loved washing and ironing – or we presumed she did – and we always had spotlessly white heavily starched sheets between numerous army blankets! It was wonderful to climb into bed between these freezing sheets – to feel them equally wonderfully warm within seconds! To this day I scorn the use of hot water bottles or electric blankets and dive naked between the sheets.

As children we never went hungry although we were always hungry! Mother used to make all our bread and with ample supplies of goats milk we used to have milk puddings every day, rice, tapioca, thick custard with whatever wild fruit in season (or preserved) blackberries, strawberries, apples including crab apples, with the pudding being made in a large 2 gallon galvanized bucket – always plenty of seconds!

When living at Middlecot and later at Avington we were too remote from church to attend regularly although mother always insisted we 'said our prayers'. At Bradpole the church was visible from our house only a few hundred yards away hence it was church three times a day on Sunday, early morning communion, afternoon Sunday school and evensong accompanied by mother and sisters. Plus once or twice every month I had to serve at communion, pump the organ and ring the bell when a single bell only was required.

For some reason I was never invited to join the choir. (I never found out why!) but I didn't lose much sleep over this thinking of choir practice, weddings, funerals etc! Also obligatory was the Sunday evening walk with mother and father until we rebelled after leaving school!

Our favourite rabbit dish was braised in the oven with liberal quantities of sliced streaky bacon, onions, carrots etc. – all nicely browned! There was always plenty of cracked eggs to be used up plus the occasional chicken found surplus from the weekend's orders, with occasional hare, mushrooms and sometimes a pheasant or partridge! As a treat we sometimes had cheddar cheese – when we used to pester mother, 'Can I have a little bit more cheese to go with this bread' – or vice-versa!

11

Mother used to make the most wonderful crab apple and blackberry jelly, always enough to last all year, we didn't need to have margarine on our bread then! Swedes, turnips, cow cabbage, kale were always available in abundance – frequently purloined from our 'thinning' activities on our way home from school!

When at Salisbury or Andover markets father used to buy up large quantities of the most unpopular bacon items, flanks, hocks etc., clearing the stalls at the end of the day and there were always literally dozens of them hanging up over the range or around walls in our kitchen. Although hard and white with salt they were always delicious once mother got to work on them.

One of her 'specials' was bacon rolls – rolled out pastry layered with bacon slices and then rolled up like a Swiss roll prior to baking in the range oven. This was always very much in demand by the farm workers who would always swap their cheese or jam sandwiches for a piece of bacon roll!

Drink, apart from milk and water, was limited to tea, or in summer as a treat, home made 'Salisbury Beer', a sort of ginger flavoured lemonade.

Pocket money was not negotiable – ½d a week each if mother could spare it. For this we could buy a small bar of Sharps creamy toffee from the oilman when he made his weekly call on Saturdays with candles, soap, paraffin etc. If we saved 5 labels/wrappers we could get a free bar – except that we had to go without our ½d that week! Occasionally we children would do a deal with each other – buy 2 bars and share them between 3 of us – giving us a spare ½d – enough to buy 5 'Brown' sweets at the village stores – although this then frequently led to rows and arguments over who had only 1 sweet last time and whose turn it wass to have only one this time! I plainly remember on one occasion when about 8 years old I saved my ½d and rushing out of school on the Friday ran to the village shop at Grately a couple of miles away where I breathlessly ordered ½d worth of raisins. Whilst I was being served, the carriers bus went past on its way to Quarley – I ran after it and managed to catch it as it let a passenger off by our school at Quarley – then hitching my usual ride on the basket, only to find there was nothing to collect when we arrived at Toplas Hill – having to drop off once again – and then getting into trouble with Nore and Glad because they had had to do my chores!

A further welcome source of income came during mushroom seasons. Father used to wake us early and we rode by cart or Ford car several miles to a field white with mushrooms where we picked 15–20 baskets, father taking them to Grately station en route to Covent Garden – leaving us to trudge back home, have breakfast and do our usual jobs before going to school! The blackberry season met with similar activity – although at rather more civilised hours!

Toplas Hill also offered a further source of income during snowy days which seemed to be more frequent in those days! The few cars around found the hill impassable so father was then in attendance with Peter (the horse) pulling cars up the hill – being rewarded with 6d, 1/– or sometimes half a crown for his efforts!

On one particularly bad winter night, father woke us up to find a blizzard raging threatening to blow off the roof. We had to arm ourselves with hammer and nails and rabbit snares and in pitch dark use them to help hold the roof down – whilst father went outside on top of the bungalow and hammered 6" nails down from the top. Fortunately all our efforts proved successful, and many more nails were applied when the storm was over!

Glad and myself were always very close, doing everything together, like on one occasion when I found (or made) a gap in the fence surrounding a nearby market garden and crept in followed by Glad. We were both happily munching strawberries when a shout told us we had been spotted. I ran wildly out of the gap in the opposite direction to our house followed by Glad who was shouting, 'Stop thief! Stop thief!' whilst trying to catch me – no chance! We made a long detour covering about 4 miles to approach home from a different direction. By the time of our arrival the irate gardener had visited mum and complained loudly but left well placated with a couple of rabbits and half a dozen eggs, and probably hoping we would do it again! No supper for us that night!

One day when I was about 7 years old, I first learnt that life could be very cruel and unfair! Our single school classroom was about 20 foot square (I checked this some 40 years later when it had been converted to a private dwelling) and housed all the pupils, about 20, aged from 5 to 14 all taught by our single teacher, a Miss Curnow. On the day in question an older boy sitting next to me 'blew off' and the resulting smell was awful. Miss Curnow had heard the noise and immediately sent him out into the playground. A few minutes later, with the awful smell still very potent, she told me to leave the room which I had to do although protesting loudly, 'It wasn't me, Teacher'. I was called back in after a few minutes by which time smell had dissipated – I was given the cane and made to stand in the corner for rest of the lesson!

Teasing was very much the order of the day between Glad and myself, and the rest of the family always knew when we had fallen out as Glad would reel out a string of girls' names,

'Joyce, Betty, Molly, Elsie, Eileen' knowing it would make me mad! (Glad reminded me of this and many of the foregoing events only a few weeks before she died over 70 years later.)

Although money was in short supply we were warmly, if unfashionably, dressed – always in khaki! Father used to barter with the different messes if they hadn't the cash, frequently returning home with quantities of army blankets, greatcoats including very good quality privately purchased officers' coats, jerseys, underclothes etc., which woollen items we were given the task of unravelling and winding into balls ready for mother to knit socks. Mother used to spend hours at her trusty old Singer sewing machine making up clothes, shirts, shorts, dresses, these lasting for years and being passed down from the older to younger as we grew up. Mother made me a special pair of long trousers, called my rabbitting trousers, for use only for that purpose, not for wearing to school!

We kept a dozen or so ferrets and I was always pestering father to go ferretting, sometimes in daytime but more often during bright moonlight nights when we could go poaching in areas not possible during the day when we could be easily seen! I used to love this, putting 'purse' nets down over every rabbit hole, then putting in the ferrets and despatching the rabbits as they escaped their burrows and became entangled in the nets.

It didn't always end happily, however, as ferrets frequently killed underground and we had to dig them out. Sometimes this wasn't possible and we had to stop up all the holes and I was given the job of visiting the site every morning and evening. I would open up the holes and catch the ferret if and when it appeared, which it invariably did – even if 7 or 8 days later. All of which I thought well worth while when father said, 'Well done, son!' I was even happier when father would

15

wake me up, usually at 2 or 3 a.m. and say, 'Come on, son – let's catch some bunnies!' No ferrets then, the weather had to be wild, windy and preferably wet – and very dark. Father had a long net about 150 yards long and he would lead the way, without making a sound, to a previously inspected site – alongside a wood or large rabbit burrow. I was armed with about twenty-five 24" long straight hazel rods, very smooth with sharp points at one end, held in a special holder like those used for arrows on my back. Father pegged one end of the net to the round and proceeded to play out the net until he reached the other end which he also pegged down. My job was to locate the lower of two cords threaded through the net at top and bottom, twist the cord around the pointed end of the rod, push it into the ground – obviously easier when it was raining – and then twist the top cord around the top end of the rod, repeating this operation every 10 or 12 yards until a net 'fence' 150 yards long by about 20" high was erected.

On reaching the end of the net where my father was waiting, I retraced my steps to the starting end, gave the net a couple of jerks to tell father I had reached the other end and we both then moved quietly away from the net with the wind blowing in our faces. We would converge on the centre and then, making a bit of noise, proceed back to the net – hopefully driving rabbits into the net where they would get entangled and could easily be located and killed. Always having to be aware that we were, in fact, poaching!

A catch of 12–15 was reckoned to be worthwhile although on one occasion we caught over 70 in one netting and had to make a total of 4 journeys to carry them home! Not forgetting our net and pegs!

We also used to make wire snares at home, twisting thin copper wire to make a strong multi-core wire with string securing one end to a wooden 'peg' with a noose at the nitty, gritty end! These we used to set on rabbit 'runs' in areas where it was not possible to ferret or set long nets. Father used to let me set a few and I was always over the moon when I found I had caught one when checking them next morning. Glad upset me by telling me that father had been out before me and put a rabbit caught in one of his snares into one of mine. I never found out whether this was true or not but one morning found I had caught a cat from a neighbouring small holding. It was absolutely terrified and I couldn't get anywhere near to release it, eventually managing to kick the peg free, when the cat raced wildly away trailing the wire and peg behind it! Father certainly hadn't put that cat in my snare!

When I was about 8 years old I remember we always looked forward to receiving the *News of the World*, in the centre of which was a half page of piano music with words which Mother and sister did their best to murder. But the lower half of the page was a serialised western story – with Sudden being the name of the hero – I don't remember whether he was a 'goody' or a 'baddy'!

In later years this was followed by turning to the back page and seeing how West Ham United had fared – particularly their amateur international centre forward, Vivian Gibbins. Plus Vic Watson, Ruffel, goalkeeper 'Ted Hufton' or similar! I don't know why I chose West Ham – to this day I have never seen them play.

Once the paper had done the rounds and been seen by all the family, it was my job to tear it into small squares, string them together on a rabbit snare and hang it on the door of the privy – heaven help me if this supply didn't last the week!

I didn't have the job of emptying the bucket – too heavy. Father did this depositing contents in a disused rabbit warren about 200 yards away – at least if not disused it soon became so! My job ended with liberally sprinkling lime onto the rabbit hole and covering it with soil, or chalk.

Glad's job was scrubbing the seat – girls' work!!!

It was whilst we were living at Middlecot that my two brothers were born, Reginald some 5 years my junior (he made a career in the RAF, and after a distinguished flying career during the war, became a peace time flyer and retired with the rank of Squadron leader) and Joey – who unfortunately died in infancy.

Excepting for Nore and Glad all my other sisters lived away from home, for the most part in 'service', living-in domestic servants. It was whilst in service that Hilly died when about 18 years old – always with the suspicion of malnutrition.

Father did enlarge the sleeping accommodation for when my elder sisters did come home, adding a wooden 'chicken house' about 8ft x 6ft to one end of the bungalow, this with inbuilt wooden bed with usual several thicknesses of army blankets to create a mattress.

Time came when I had to visit the school dentist at his Andover surgery, which I did sitting on the carrier of Eve's bike, making the return journey of about 8 miles after having nine teeth removed!

When I was about 8½ years old my father bought an old Model T Ford, reconditioned the engine and cut off the back, building on what would now be called a pick-up truck back. To my sorrow he then sold Peter as horse and cart were redundant.

Just over 12 months later father's business received a hammer blow from which it never recovered and neither did father. Leaving one Saturday morning with a full load of chickens as usual, he returned late in the afternoon with the

School photograph of author,
1930.

load intact. Glad and I were in the kitchen and heard father
and mother talking in their bedroom with mother sobbing
uncontrollably. We later learnt that when father made his
normal calls all the messes told him they had suffered huge pay
cuts, and were unable to buy anything in future and would not
be able to pay off their existing accounts, adding up to
thousands of pounds. They all told father to call with his
empty car the following week when they would see what they
could lay their hands on in recompense, obviously in no way
helping in any financial sense. Father made several trips
returning with all sorts of goods ranging from clothes,
blankets, footwear etc. to cases of corned beef, tinned foods,
soap, candles etc. Some of this he managed to sell to dealers at

Salisbury and Andover markets but we remember this as being the very first time we had tasted tinned peaches, pears and pineapples!

Father had to sell everything – smallholding, bungalow and all stock, and on my tenth birthday, family and all belongings were loaded onto a large farm wagon and moved to Avington, near Winchester, my father to work as farm worker and part time gamekeeper. With Nor and Glad, I went to school (by school bus!) at Itchen Abbas, a new building with 4/5 classrooms and head mistress with her assistant and four 17–18 year old junior teachers.

Our new home was directly off the farmyard with its permanently growing 12–15ft high dung heap! I soon got to know all the carters and their horses, including one carter with only one arm, still looking after the horse which had bitten the other one off several years previously! At weekends and during holidays I was always out with one carter or another, a matter of choice not of necessity as had been the case previously, this having instilled in me the desire and willingness to always be on the go and not shirk hard work – something which has never waivered.

My willingness to work, and work hard, led to me always being the first in line if extra help was needed on this very large farm, eventually being paid, particularly during hay making and harvesting, when I could earn 6d a day enabling me to proudly give mother anything up to 3/– a week! This often meant getting up at 5.00a.m., get to the field by 6.00a.m., arriving back home at about 8.00p.m. and not feeling exploited as long as I could give mother some money at the end of the week.

My job consisted of leading a pair of horses, stopping against a stook of corn sheaves whilst they were loaded and then taking the loaded cart to the corn rick – collecting the empty cart previously delivered. Occasionally I was required to get on the rick being formed and place sheaves in required position. When hay making, 'sweeps' were used to collect hay from the field to the rick, backing horses to empty the 'sweep' before collecting a further load.

Going into the farmyard one Saturday morning I was told by one of my favourite carters that one of his horses had died of poisoning during the night and he was waiting for the 'knackers lorry' to arrive to collect the corpse. When they arrived they tied ropes to the rear legs of the horse and attempted to winch it out of the stable, but the corpse had swollen so much that it would not go through the door, whereupon knives were used to cut into the body allowing vast clouds of foul smelling 'gases' to emerge. The body reduced sufficiently so that it could easily be pulled through the door and loaded into the lorry.

Whilst I was at Itchen Abbas school, I was the only pupil out of some 200 to be put forward for my 11 plus exam although only 10½ years old. Travelling by myself on the bus, my very first such journey, I was sent to Winchester where I had to find my own way to the great hall at Winchester College where I found 150 or so other hopefuls.

I was completely overwhelmed by it all, with no recollection later of what took place, my only memory is of being concerned as to how I was going to meet Eve who had been despatched to meet me and take me home to Avington, on her bike, after the exam. Needless to say several weeks later I learnt that I had not passed, in common with most of the other aspirants, only four having been successful!

Once again I was to find how unjust life could be – during playtime at school, one of the older boys, 14 years old and much bigger than me, knocked Glad off a fallen tree in the field near the playground, cutting her leg and making her cry. I was lean, wiry and very strong so set about this boy and beat him up causing him to report me to the head teacher, followed by my receiving the cane and having to stand in the corner of the classroom! My one concern was that I would be barred from going on the school's annual outing a week or so later, this year by open top charabanc to Highcliffe near Bournemouth. I did go, and this was my first sight of the sea. Just before Christmas we also went to the annual school Christmas party where we were disappointed that we did not get an apple and an orange as we had always received at Quarley Christmas party!

Father's 'gamekeepering' had been restricted to shooting a few rabbits and 'wild' pheasants, no rearing game, and all catches had to be handed over to the farm bailiff. On my eleventh birthday (I was later told the date was purely incidental) we found ourselves on a farm wagon again, this time to Bradpole in Dorset, my father to work in the local Pymore Rope Works. My sisters were also required to work there, a condition for occupying the three bedroomed 'tied' house. The wages were at least steady if very poor. For the very first time we lived in a house with a bathroom, no running hot water of course that had to be carried upstairs from the wood fired wash boiler in the kitchen! There was an outdoor flush toilet, under cover but it used to freeze up in the winter!

Weekly (sometimes daily) wash was done by using the wash boiler in the kitchen, filling it from the nearby tap in the earthenware sink and emptying the boiler by hand onto the front garden! No washing powder in those days, soap flakes if Mother could afford it, otherwise Sunlight soap on the scrubbing board, plenty of soda and the inevitable Robin starch!

Apart from collecting firewood from hedgerows we had very little work to do. No chickens to feed, just gardening (a very big front garden) and the weekly jaunt to the village garage to take and collect the 'accumulator' for our newly acquired wireless! This latter proved very popular especially with neighbours who used to congregate on our front lawn to listen to cricket commentaries. Father used to open all the windows! A few years later the house was fitted with electricity enabling us to dispense with the oil lamps and candles, we could do our homework in the dark evenings, plus board games, cards and reading anything we could lay our hands on.

Glad and I went to school at Bradpole with three teachers and three classrooms. The head teacher was Miss Daryl Reed who was quite a character, cycling to work in all weathers from her bungalow at West Bay with her dog trailing behind on its lead. Without me being aware that I was particularly 'bright' I soon found Miss Reed giving me extra attention and homework! I was always very interested in arithmetic (no mathematics in those days!) English and Geography, but had no time at all for history, had no interest in kings and queens, dates etc. and so made no effort in that direction thinking them irrelevant! I had the consolation of never being called 'teacher's pet', my fellow students being only too well aware of my physical prowess to take chances and tease me!

I was particularly keen on mental arithmetic, spelling and essays, compositions as they used to be called. Miss Reed was always embarrassing me by asking me to recite my 'composition' in front the class, later relenting and getting one of my classmates to take over this task, not easy as clarity of writing was never one of my strong points, rather surprisingly as Mother wrote a beautiful script and was always being pressurised to write prefaces in prayer and hymn books by the local vicar.

Around this time I became obsessed with football, in fact I wore football boots to school at all times, replacing worn studs with strips cut from old motor cycle tyres. What I lacked in skill was compensated for by my strength, fitness and enthusiasm, born out by the fact that if I was not one of those chosen to select the team, I was invariably the first one selected! Only a couple of us had football boots, most of the boys wore hob nailed boots. I've still got the dents in my shin bones to prove it! I never did find out where the real leather football came from, but it was in use for years, long after we ran out of spares to repair the inside with bicycle tube patches but we could always get plenty of pigs' bladders as one of the boys' father had an abattoir in the village which he now runs.

I still had a tendency to get into scrapes, one complaint to mother from a lady when they met at church was because she was sure it was me she disturbed scrumping apples in her orchard (it was!) for which I got a right telling off. Another visitor was the mother of a 14 year old boy who had left school and jeered at me because I was still wearing shorts – two black eyes and a swollen mouth later he had confessed to his mum, resulting in her visiting mine! There were twin brothers in my class at school and because there were two of them they overstepped the mark one day and in the resultant fight both succumbed, twins or not! There was a sequel to this many years later in Assam, North East India when serving with the forgotten Fourteenth. On a train journey we had to get off and bed down for the night in nearby jungle; one of those travelling on the same train had not expected to spend the night away from his unit and so didn't have a blanket or mosquito net, the latter being an absolute essential, so we shared mine. When it got light in the morning he recognised me, and me him later, as one of the twins!

One of the school lessons I enjoyed most was the afternoon spent tending our own individual garden plots behind the village hall under the guidance of a local market gardener. Every year we were all entered in 'the best kept garden' competition which I won every time I entered and had then to collect a certificate and prize at the annual Bridport Chrysanthemum show – I still have certificates to prove it! Mr Brake, the gardener in question, soon asked me to work for him which I did from 12 years old – pay 3d an hour – meaning that every week I was able to give mother at least 1/– increasing to 2/– or 3/– later when two other villagers made similar offers! Both these other employers used to give me tea and cakes, me welcoming both the break in work and the refreshments!

When I left school at 14 years old completely without any real qualifications except a letter of commendation from Miss Reed, I worked as many hours as I could (normally 4–5 hours a day) at gardening, then at 4d an hour for a week or so. I then obtained a full time job as errand boy at a grocer's shop, one of a national chain in Bridport, wage 7/– per week taking charge of the shop delivery box tricycle, a large box between the front wheels which weighed about 1 cwt when empty and anything up to 3–4 cwt when filled with customers' orders for delivery to their homes in Bridport and surrounding villages. Sometimes it was impossible to ride, I had to push the trike up even the slightest of hills and there were plenty of those around Bridport. At least the Walls ice cream trikes of similar design carried a means of refreshing oneself!!

My predecessor was promoted into serving in the shop but after two weeks I was given his job and he reverted to errand boy, me getting a raise to 10/– a week, he retaining the rise he had been given. We had very long hours and hard work: start 7.00a.m., half an hour for lunch – close shop at 6.00p.m. – leaving about 6.30p.m. after scrubbing counters, floors. Half day on Thursday – when I could play my beloved football, soon graduating to the Bridport Thursday team!

I had always been very keen and good at mental arithmetic, which stood me in good stead at work as I became very adept at adding up the cost of customers' purchases, there were no till rolls, just add up and put the cash in an open drawer, giving change as necessary. This ability used to impress the customers who would sometimes embarrass me by declining to be served by other staff some of whom were old enough to be my parents! I was very naïve as to what the shop had to offer, I can remember causing huge laughs on one occasion, a woman ordering 3 tins of corned beef and nearly fainting when I plonked 3 x 7lb tins on the counter instead of the 3 x 12oz tins she wanted!

There was a sequel to this when, a couple of weeks later the same lady returned accompanied by her sister, and again asked for 3 'small' tins of corned beef, whereupon her sister said 'get 2 for me'. I suggested it would be far cheaper if they shared a 7lb tin (cost 3/6d) when they would get 3½lbs each for 1s 9d as against paying 3s 1½d each for less than 4lb for 5 small tins. After due discussion they agreed, asking me to open the large tin and cut its contents in half. Another small argument, 'I don't want all the fat end and none of the jelly/lean end', this was easily solved, I cut it in half lengthways! Everyone was happy I thought, not counting on the fact that the manager had been watching, and far from commending me said, 'Don't ever do that again!' explaining that after buying the 3 small tins, she would have bought ¼lb or ½lb of other cooked meat

– tongue, brisket beef, brawn, sliced ham or even ham off the bone! But her husband would have to put up with corned beef in his sandwiches for the next 3 to 4 weeks, and if all our customers took similar action we could just as well close down our cooked meat counter! A case of taking salesmanship one step too far!

Needless to say I didn't explain the advantage of bulk buying to a customer a few days later who asked for a jar of jam, and wasn't amused when I offered her a 7lb jar (for 3s 6d) instead of the 12oz jar (10½d) requested, after all I wasn't on commission!

Very small amounts were frequently requested simply because they couldn't afford more, 2oz of margarine, 2oz of cheese, 2 rashers of bacon, 2 sausages etc. 3 cracked eggs, and ¼lb of broken biscuits were commonly asked for.

Also many customers had large families and were on 'Poor Law' producing 10/- or 12/- vouchers listing varying amounts for different types of food – 6/- for groceries, 1/6 for vegetables, 1/6 for meat etc., and we were not allowed to deviate although regularly requested to put in a 2d packet of 5 Woodbine cigarettes instead of the 1lb sugar (price 2¼d) listed!

I always remembering a little boy asking for a packet of Woodbines whose mother had told him 'If they won't give you fags, get a bar of Sunlight soap'!

Goods were delivered daily from the local railway station and it was my job with the errand boy to unload and take them to various stores, the cellar (no refrigerators in those days!) or a room on one of the two floors above the shop. This included 2 cwt sacks of sugar and soda, (2 lots of stairs!). Crates of cheese (1¾ cwt), cases of corned beef, canned fruit etc., sides of bacon, casks of butter etc., down to the cellar. The delivery men were always marvelling at my ability to handle these loads, equally the shop manager who showed me a way to lift a bag of sugar (2 cwt) without overstraining myself. The trick was to tie the two 'ears' of the bag together to form a firm handle this obviously helping when bags had to be stacked two high. The errand boy (Doug) and myself soon found a way to put this to monetary advantage Doug would tell the drivers, who seemed to change frequently, that I could lift 2 cwt a foot off the ground with one hand. No difficulty in getting them to bet 3d or 6d that I couldn't, which I did without effort, merely by standing astride the bag on two boxes of butter or canned fruit! This within a few weeks of starting work!

Mother used to give me back 6d a week pocket money so extra earnings as above were most welcome enabling us to have a occasional 3d each way on a horse at a nearby bookies' then entirely illegal. I well remember having a joint bet with Doug on a horse called 'Quashed' in the Oaks, it must have been around 1934, we put 6d each way, really lashing out! And it won at 33–1! Doug collected the winnings and when we worked it out, found we had been underpaid by ½d. Doug went back and confronted the bookie who didn't have ½d so reluctantly gave Doug (who threatened to use another bookie!) 1d which made it easier to split between us!

I had always had a secret ambition to be a newspaper reporter, so when a footballing friend (who worked in a solicitors office) said he was going to learn shorthand I decided to join him, for nearly 18 months attending private tuition class (only 6 of us) held by Mr Stephens who also happened to be the Chief Clerk at Pymore Mills.

I did reasonably well with the theoretical side, achieving 25–30 words a minute at dictation speed. When we were about 6/7 weeks into the 'speed' phase it all came to an abrupt end when Mr Stephens went off the rails and disappeared, being found two days later in a nearby river. We were all quite adamant we were not responsible, after all we did lose all the half-crown (2/6) fees we had paid every time we entered his front room! On the other hand, we couldn't find anyone else willing to take us on!

I had only been working for a few months when one morning the shop manager took a phone call from dad's workplace, Pymore Mills, saying my father had been taken ill and I was to get a taxi and collect him from a certain shed where I found him lying on a heap of sacks and ropes. It turned out father had had a severe heart attack and never worked again.

I was further upset to find out that Nor and Glad were working at looms only a few yards away and only learnt of father's attack when they arrived home from work about 6.15p.m. That's' how workers were treated in those days!

Although Father was never able to work again, we kept our 'tied' house as it was the female labour the mill wanted!

When I was 15 the manager instructed me in the running of the shop, paperwork and books to be maintained, involving all aspects, takings, banking, re-ordering, weekly summaries etc. and a few months later aged 15½ years, I was given the job of managing the shop when the manager took his annual holidays. I had no problems in taking and costing stock at the start and finish of the two weeks, the first late on Saturday after the shop had closed, then on Sunday afternoon when the manager returned. Fortunately the figures agreed, always doubtful as with 'open' tills it would have been easy for any of the 8 staff all very much older than myself to have helped themselves and so put me in dead trouble. Also, all bags, wrappers etc. were charged into the shop at the price of the product, hence 56lb box of butter had to produce 113 x ½lb packets, 2 cwt bag of sugar to 226 x 1lb bags!

In the following years this became a regular job, relief managing both the Bridport shop and those in other towns, Weymouth, Exeter, Plymouth etc., when managers were on leave, ill or 'between managers'. I received an extra 10/– a week for this – plus 25/– lodging allowance when away from Bridport. One Sunday afternoon I was contacted by my manager who had been instructed by the chief inspector from head office to send me to Weymouth branch by 9.00a.m. next morning. On arrival I was met by very surprised manager (whom I knew, having relieved him the previous year) but before I could tell him what little I knew the chief inspector arrived and took him into the tiny rear office. A few minutes later the manager emerged with outdoor clothes on and departed.

I was then called in, was told the manager had been sacked and I was to take over until further notice, my first job being to take and value stock, not easy when customers were still being served. In the evening one of the staff gave me the sacked manager's home address only a couple of hundred yards away in an adjacent street. Needless to say I was most surprised to find this was a grocer's shop which, on being invited in, I discovered was like a smaller version of our own shop – most of the fittings, scales, slate butter slabs etc. having been found a new home from the 'parent' shop as had numerous customers, particularly a number of small hotels, boarding houses whose custom was very necessary if the main shop was to prove viable. No legal action was ever taken – obviously because of the bad publicity which would follow if pay and hours were highlighted in open court.

When I was 17 years old we reached the final of the major

local football cup, The Edwards Charity Cup, when I was unfortunate enough to give away the penalty which lost us the final against Beaminster then a Dorset Division one team, boasting several county players including an ex pro player. I did, however, get a very favourable report in the following edition of the local paper. I was due to take over as captain elect in the 1937/38 season but I was never able to take up this position as I was permanently transferred to the Cowlin Street, Exeter branch. I carried on playing football in midweek in Exeter, joining a team at St Lukes College. A few weeks after starting with them I was asked to attend for trials with Exeter City at St James Park where I did reasonably well for the 45 minutes I played, being told I would be contacted to take further trials in the near future. Once again fate intervened as I was sent to open a new shop at Horfield in Bristol. I was first told I could take over permanently but after a few weeks a new manager turned up from a shop in Wales, it being realised that as I was single I was more useful as relief manager, resulting in several relief jobs at other Bristol shops including Weston Super Mare where the shop was closing for a few weeks whilst it was being re-developed.

It was while I was at the Horfield shop that I met Gladys, daughter of one of the customers, whom I started dating regularly. Then aged 19, I told my inspector that I was thinking of settling down and getting married but could only do this if offered a permanent shop. He tried to dissuade me, one of the things he said has always remained with me: 'If I want to employ a manager or any other shop worker I have only to go to any pit head in Wales and I could engage the first half dozen men to come up!' My immediate response to this was that if the employment position was that bad on no account would I ever take a shop in Wales.

Gladys and I on our wedding day, 1938.

We decided to get married as my prospects looked good and tied the knot on 6th June 1938 at Horfield church having been sent to Weston Super Mare to open the renovated shop a week previously. We went straight to the two rooms I had rented at 6/– a week at Weston Super Mare, having to spend our honeymoon on the train journey on Bank Holiday Monday, starting work next morning at 7.00a.m. For several weeks I was in heaven, my own shop at last, only to be stunned after 3 weeks when Bill Hyde, who I knew as the manager of the Evesham branch, arrived and took over as manager.

However I had cast my die and there was nothing I could do but carry on as first hand with resultant drop in pay of 10/– per week and 25/– lodging allowance. After paying 6/– a week rent making ends meet was only possible by my being able to buy certain things cheaper, cracked eggs, bacon ends, hocks etc. and special offers!

Once again I started playing football, this time for a local mid-week team who included in their ranks a certain Bill Andrews of Somerset and England cricket fame, a real rough, tough guy who gave more hard knocks than he took!

After repeatedly accosting the inspector re getting my own shop, in December I was told during a visit by the Chief Inspector that he had a shop for me and I was to report to Tonypandy the following Monday. The only thing I knew was that Tonypandy was in Wales and was where Tommy Farr the boxer came from! Remembering what I had previously been told about jobs in Wales I flatly refused the offer. One thing leading to another resulted in me being given instant dismissal, no notice, pay or holiday pay after nearly 6 years service.

Having collected my cards (this on a Wednesday) I went

into a branch of David Grieg Grocers about 50 yards away and was instantly engaged and told to start at their very big store (50–60 staff) at Castle Street, Bristol on the following Monday morning at 5/– a week more than I had been getting! This just gave me time to go to Bristol and rent a single large room in a house just off Portland Square, then a reasonably good area of Bristol, not what one would call it nowadays! We moved on the Saturday, I started work on the Monday and was immediately given a responsible job – first hand on the 'provision' (cooked meats, bacon, cheese, butter etc.) counter. On the Tuesday after starting work there I was entrusted with the job of banking the previous days takings, several thousands of pounds. Presumably because 'Country Boys' were always honest!

The next week was that before Christmas and involved working 14–15 hours a day and no half day that week. Wednesday, the day before Christmas Eve, we started work at 6.00a.m. working right through until 3.00a.m. on Christmas Eve, the 30 or so male staff members working with me in the very large cellar making up bacon joints, slicing bacon, packing butter etc. We were all relieved when the manager popped his head round the door and told us to pack up. We were all trooping over to the single sink (cold water) in the corner when he re-appeared and said, 'Everybody back on the job by 6.00a.m.!'

No one bothered to go home, snatching what sleep we could on empty sugar sacks etc. We couldn't complain, after all we had all been promised a 10/– Christmas Box (no overtime pay then!) Apparently I had impressed the manager as early in the new year I was given a 5/– a week rise.

On Saturdays, it was my job to stand on the pavement outside the shop with window raised open, the road was impassable to traffic, very few cars about, no horses and carts or deliveries on Saturdays, and the trams did not run past the shop so the road and pavements were packed with people. I had to select something from the huge display we had previously put in the window, a pack of sliced bacon, a bacon joint, a couple of pounds (a string) of sausages, weigh it, shout out the price, 'sliced gammon – 8d', 'sausages 6d' etc. – which offer would be immediately snapped up – whereupon I threw it to one of a dozen staff inside the shop who would wrap it and take the money. 7–8 hours of this and I was clapped out waiting for 9.00 to come so we could close and get down to some easy work scrubbing counters etc! Which we could do by 11.00 on a good day!

Sundays were spent visiting my wives' relatives, apart from her parents, there were numerous aunties, cousins etc. where we were always made very welcome for both Sunday lunch and teas, both of which were very welcome. Especially as we were invariably given cakes, sponges etc. to take home. I did make the mistake of telling one cousin that I loved watercress, this then being the staple diet offered on all subsequent visits! We normally walked to our relatives' homes, frequently 5 or 6 miles, then enjoyed the luxury of a tram ride home!

Mother was becoming increasingly concerned about father's health and was anxious for me to get a job nearer them. Eventually father obtained a job for me as an insurance agent at Bridport although at considerably less pay than I was then getting, especially as when I gave in my notice I was offered a further 10/– a week, then 15/– to stay. Mother and father had arranged for us to rent a cottage at 7/– a week, and rather than upset them further we decided to move! My district covered a wide area of West Dorset from Charmouth to Beaminster, Cattistock, Dorchester down to the coast. My means of transport an aged bicycle! A three speed would have helped on those hills, but money wouldn't stretch to that. Taking this job was a big mistake, I simply was not cut out to be an insurance agent and hated it. I needed to have physical tasks, not chatting people up, most of whom had a hard enough job to get by without taking on 3d or 6d a week policies. I must have been the worst agent ever. Although I had a wide circle of acquaintances from both my years in the shop and football, it went very much against the grain to approach them. I was given virtually no training, the area manager joined me on my rounds for two days, during the first week not getting any new 'business' despite all his efforts to do so, and any business I obtained only went to replace 'lost' business which occurred every time a policy matured or was surrendered.

The War Years

When war looked inevitable I was in the first age group due to be called up in August. At that time Glad was pregnant and I managed to obtain a 3 month postponement, then a further 3 months, during which time Glad gave birth prematurely to a stillborn son in Bridport hospital. This had a devastating affect on her. I was eventually called up early in 1940. I joined the Fifth Dorsets at Frome in Somerset, being posted to 'M' (Militia) company with 200 or so others. We were first billeted in empty houses, sleeping about 15–20 to a room, for the first few days on the bare floor boards with 3 blankets! 2–3 days later we were 'marched' with all our kit (including rather hotch-potch uniforms!) to Frome market where we were all issued with mattress covers (the army called them palliasses) ushered to a huge heap of straw and told to stuff the palliasses as full as we could as these would be our beds for the foreseeable future. We were then marched to a tented village at the top of the town, our home for the next 3 months. Within days we were subjected to heavy snowfalls, there was no heating except in one large tent used as mess room, only cold water for washing and the toilets, well I had better not elaborate except that many chaps quickly made private 'arrangements' with local families to use their facilities!

Everyone realised it was no good complaining so we all buckled down and rather enjoyed the very intense training – drills, route marches, firing ranges. The food was plentiful if not very varied or appetising, Soya link sausages, bully beef, beans, supplemented by local vegetables, with rice as 'afters' every day. We soon grew to dislike the latter, no problem as there was one chap (name of Fido, a gypsy) who loved it! He sat at the table near the door and we emptied our plates onto his which he soon despatched, using two spoons at a time! Likewise another chap who really liked Soya link sausages!

Company orders one day instructed about 20 of us to report to the local drill hall to a certain corporal. We had no idea what for, except it was some type of physical exercise. We knew what this was as soon as the corporal appeared, he had no nose, it had been pushed back into his face, his ears were monstrous appendages and he couldn't speak properly or 'legibly'. It turned out he had been army boxing champion for several years and it showed.

Needless to say, he had little success in getting us to sign on for his boxing squad despite promising special privileges, no guard duties etc. except for 3 chaps who had dabbled and thought it a bit of a laugh!

I eventually joined the football squad, also volunteering for cross county running. Both were good choices and we also had certain privileges, as for boxing. It was whilst playing football here that I met Ernie Hopkins who was later to become a great friend in civvy street, dying in 1998 nearly 59 years after we first met.

Chaps from all over the country were in this first batch, London, Bristol and Cornwall being well represented and despite our differing back grounds many close friendships were formed, some still going strong long after the war.

Every Saturday morning we were all assembled for 'Adjutants' parade – this to demonstrate what results the intense training given during previous week had achieved. If all went well we were dismissed at about 11.30 giving those who came from Bristol (including myself), just time to catch the 12.15 train home. Later it could entail a fast run to the station relying on our pals to take our rifles and equipment back to our tents!

After 8–9 weeks of 'M' company training we were all allocated to different platoons (about 30 in a platoon) most to the rifle companies but some to specialist platoons, mortars, signals, medical, carrier. For some reason I could never fathom I was sent to the motorised carrier platoon, small open top lightweight 'tanks', together with 20 or so others, all of whom were fully fledged car/lorry drivers before being called up. I was the only one with no driving qualifications at all! Actually this turned out to be to my advantage, being given intensive individual driving instruction which I picked up quite quickly, whereas those with driving experience had to 'un-learn' some of their skills due to the big difference between driving a vehicle with 4 wheels, and a carrier with two tracks, where 'steering' was a mixture between 'steering' and 'braking'. The end result was that in later years I was teaching some of the car/lorry drivers how to drive carriers!

After 3–4 weeks training over the wide expanses of Salisbury Plain, we carried out several 'exercises' where we had to spend nights in the open using our tarpaulins and camouflage nets to create makeshift tents, all really good fun! After one such exercise, we were all given numerous inoculations then went out that night on further exercise. We had all bedded down for the night on a piece of scrubland just off a main road and I was one of two sentries on guard at about 2.00a.m. when we were 'found' by a despatch rider who gave our officer orders requiring us to pack up and return to Frome immediately. We were then given a further hour to prepare to move – which we did, merely following a D.R. in convoy with not a clue as to our destination. On nearing Newbury we were halted for a couple of hours, moved off again, arriving at St. Albans in Hertfordshire late in the evening, taking over several empty houses in Sandpit Lane with our carriers parked on the verge opposite (usual sentries posted!)

We were told to be on parade at 6.00a.m. next day – then marched to Radlett aerodrome, given pick axes and shovels and instructions to dig trenches and erect sandbag gun emplacements around the airfield and nearby aeroplane factory. This was the norm for the next 9–10 days: up at 6.00a.m., march to Radlett, work until 5.00p.m., march back to St. Albans. After the first few days a lot of us had vaccine fever and so were excused digging, having to spend several days sleeping on the floor with raging fever and looking after each other; whoever was fittest had to walk half a mile to the cookhouse to collect 'Dixies' of tea and whatever food was on offer – although food was the last thing on our minds. As soon as we were fit enough – back to digging!

Company orders were still being posted outside company HQ (½ mile away) every day and we were expected to read them every night after we returned from Radlett so we arranged a rota whereby two or three chaps read them and passed on any relevant orders. One such order stated that our weekly bundles of clean washing – shirts, pants, vests, socks, towels etc. must be collected before stores closed at 6.00p.m. at which time we were still marching back and so were unable to collect.

Nearly all of us were 'put on charge' – no excuses accepted – and we were all given 7 days 'Jankers', i.e. confined to 'barracks', and had to carry out 2–3 hours of fatigues every day! I spent the only 'Jankers' I was ever given scrubbing the floors in the battalion HQ, these having been the central library reading room before the war! Not a lot of time to do anything else every day except sleep (if not on sentry duty!)

When work at Radlett was finished really intensive training continued and we were all issued with new arms, the majority with rifles but some including myself ending up with American Tommy guns, having to borrow rifles to do arms drill as it was not possible with Tommy guns! We were also issued with 5 rounds of ammunition each – not of much use as the shortest 'burst' of fire possible with this automatic Tommy gun was 6 or 7 rounds – unless you only had 5!!

It was a privilege to be in the carriers-room to carry extra water and rations, somewhere to sleep in the dry when raining and NO marching. On one very hot day when we were travelling behind marching troops we went about ½ mile until we caught up with the marching troops, then stopped for 10–15 minutes to let them get ahead again. We were travelling through Hitchen. Every time we stopped, particularly in the less well off area of the town, we were showered with cold drinks, tea, cakes, sweets etc. Stopping outside a large house with huge brass plates naming the occupier, we were approached by a very elegant young lady carrying a tray with glasses, accompanied by a very posh gent, obviously her father, carrying a large jug of water.

'Would you like some water?' she asked the corporal standing in the front. He in turn winked at me standing in the back and asked, 'Can we do with any water?' Whereupon I removed the heavy iron panel alongside me exposing the engine, took off the radiator cap and said, 'Yes please,' proceeding to top up the radiator one glass at a time (it took 7 or 8 glasses) as the jug was too tall to go beneath the engine cowling! I often thought later how this must have upset her but at the time I could only think of the very different gifts given us at previous stops.

We had very little time off when at St. Albans, only on Sundays after church parade at the cathedral when we used to visit local canteens and Verulam Park if weather permitted. We did find a cake shop in the town where one of the counter hands had a husband serving overseas and arrangements were made for one of our gang to call on Friday afternoons and buy 6d worth of 'stale cakes' which turned out to be 35–40 cakes taken straight out of the window!

After pay parade, usually on Friday, we were introduced by one of our sergeants to Crown & Anchor – a dice game with Crown & Anchor on opposite sides of the dice – hearts, clubs, diamonds and spades on others – with a matching board, this being a piece of cloth – the game being against KRR – Kings Rules & Regulations – The Army Bible!

With the sergeant running the board all you had to do was place your money on the segment selected, winning if the dice matched it, this only being rolled with bets all in position. It didn't take long for us to realise that if 10 or 15 were playing the sergeant would slow down and stop altogether – but if only 2 or 3 playing he would keep going as he invariably won! After he had fleeced us for several weeks one of our mates, a lovely amiable Cornishman called Dennis Matthews whose parents had a large market garden near Penzance and who apart from being our 'banker' shared a large parcel with us every week, Cornish pasties, tooth paste, shoe polish, soap 'Blanco' etc., and who also did not gamble, decided enough was enough and set out one afternoon to break the sergeant. He had no chance of doing so as odds were 6 to 1 against. After losing over £60 (a fortune to all of us!) he told the sergeant he was broke – whereupon the sergeant gave him the 'board' with the comment that he wouldn't have the heart to play again. Matt promptly took the board and burnt it in the combustion stove in the middle of the room.

Whilst at St. Albans, we had 4–5 days training on the firing ranges at Bisley, having to drive our carriers through Windsor where we had great difficulty in travelling up the main cobbled street outside the castle, finishing by driving with one track on the pavement, the other in the gutter! After spending a day on the field firing area firing live ammunition we spent the rest of the week manning the range whilst other units trained. Scattered over the range were 20 or so 'firing points', concrete positions below ground level facing away from approaching troops, each with a pull wire attached to a target (figure of a man) positioned a few yards in front. On a high central tower at the back of the range was the range firing officer connected by phone to each of the firing points. As advancing troops approached the officer called 'up six' etc., when pulling the wire raised the target which was lowered when the target had received 2 or 3 hits in marked areas, the troops then proceeding to the next target. We found out that whilst the officer could speak to all points and we to him, he had no way of telling which point was calling him, this led to several days when Brigadier General Smythe BART called him, berating him for not knowing his job – bumbling nincompoop – and not a clue as to the source!

A few changes of accent and the rank of the caller drove him to a right state, at the end of the second day he addressed us all asking us to name the culprits. No way, as even we didn't know unless we were the guilty parties! Our 'Colonel Bloggs' certainly won that battle!

Via the grapevine, we learnt that when stopped at Newbury, we had actually been en route to France, being diverted to St.

Albans when the top brass decided against sending in further units. Lucky us or Dunkirk would have been looming! Shortly afterwards we entrained complete with carriers and found ourselves next morning at Dover – right in the middle of the Battle of Britain! Thank God Jerry never came, as with only 4 months training we were the frontline troops! All with 5 rounds of ammunition, although we could probably have obtained replacements for any used had we still been around!!

I was given my first stripe (Lance Corporal – extra 6d a day) shortly after arriving at Dover and put in charge of a carrier – crew of 3 – half of my extra pay having to be allocated to Glad!

For a few days we were stationed in South Front Barracks built into the cliffs on the west side of Dover – all below ground with 3 long rooms each housing about 60 soldiers with a single window facing the sea. The snag was that over 350 steps had to be negotiated to reach our barrack room at the bottom of the shaft! Our carriers were parked around the parade ground some quarter of a mile away and we were supposed to be a rapid response unit. It took nearly half an hour to reach our carriers. Also, there was only one single track road leading up from the town to the barrack square – both these facts were pointed out to the CO and we were promptly re-located on the Canterbury Road out of Dover with us in houses and carriers spread around adjacent county cricket and football grounds. This delighted us as it meant we had our own cookhouse catering for about 35 men instead of the battalion cookhouse for 900 plus!

As all the children and most of the women had been evacuated and civilian rations had been allocated to the shops based on the pre-war population we could buy many extras (if money was available) to supplement army issue and we fed very well. The main London to Dover railway ran beside our billets and we used to detail men to walk along the line collecting coal for use in billets and cookhouse, with many of the train drivers throwing out coal when they saw us collecting!

A week after we moved our orderly room received a direct hit from cross channel shelling, no one was hurt but we were deducted 9d each from our next pay, 'Barrack Room Damage' to pay for repairs. This being the first of many such payments!

Our training was mainly aimed towards getting us to know the surrounding countryside, familiarising ourselves to the extent that upon being given a map reference we could immediately make our way there in the shortest possible time. We all quickly became very good map readers, and myself in particular as I was keen to impress as a Carrier NCO!

This invariably led us through farms and orchards resulting in company orders being posted prohibiting us from picking fruit from trees or digging up vegetables. We strictly observed this order but unfortunately our carriers frequently nudged trees and turned round in fields when we felt obliged to pick up the fruit and potatoes etc. to stop them rotting!

There were many hilarious happenings, not all contrived, when out on these training jaunts. One such was when I was driving a heavy Norton motor cycle with attached sidecar (with Bren gun mounted in front) down a horse track between two woods of hazel nut trees having to balance the machine on the two 'banks' created by the horse track in the centre and cart tracks on either side.

Suddenly I lost all control, falling forward over the petrol tank, the combination shot off the track and ran into a large bunch of hazel saplings bending them down and leaving us stranded some 5ft–6ft up in the air. After some cajoling and

Carrier platoon, 5th Dorsets, at Dover, 1940.
Author third from right, back row.

amid much laughter the following troops used their machetes to cut us down. Then we found the nuts holding the through bolt securing the footrests had shaken loose allowing both foot rests to collapse.

On another occasion, again driving the combination I had as my gunner (sitting behind Bren gun in the chair) a real character, Frankie Gardner, who had endeared himself to all on our very first parade. Asked by the NCO to give our names, initials and what the latter stood for – Frankie said 'Gardner, F.B.,' followed by 'F****** B******, and I am'. A lovely chap who had been a bit of a rogue before joining up. He regaled us one night with his 'first' experience of being banged up in Horfield prison – 'I stood on the top bunk and looking out of the barred window and thought this is not a bad view – I could just see the tops of the buses going down Gloucester

Road!' Although he was a bit of a thief we could leave money, soap etc. on our beds without second thoughts! The 'chair' had a lever allowing the chair wheel to be engaged or disengaged. Approaching a corner, Frankie suddenly disengaged the gear resulting in us careering through a hedge into a ploughed field! No damage, just a lot of sweat getting it back on the road! Both events caused some raised eyebrows when the MT officer read the accident report.

One day travelling down a sunken single track road at about 30 miles an hour, we were suddenly confronted by a long bonnet Humber staff car rounding a bend about 40 yards away. No problem in them stopping but carriers needed 50–60 yards to stop, we did, but only after climbing up over the front of the long bonnet with the officer alongside the driver straining backwards to avoid also being crushed. Another 1/6d barrack room damages, no charge as the officer was off route – we weren't!

Farmers generally were willing to offer fruit, vegetables, eggs etc. especially if we agreed not to drive over their fields or orchards which we were entitled to do! We were given cheap entry into the local cinema once a week. We used to buy cooked pigs trotters (a favourite with all of us) before entering the flicks and derived more amusement from throwing bones up to where officers were sitting than we did from the films! Life was pretty grim, anything for a laugh! Due to over use of cleaning powder and starch by the laundry doing our washing for a couple of weeks we all had 'Dhobies Itch' – a very sore rash between our thighs and privates and nothing seemed to get rid of it. Some of our lads who lived in London managed to get 24 hour passes at weekends. After one such leave, one returned and assured one of our more unpopular sergeants who had been badly affected that he had obtained some liniment to cure it. The sergeant applied it liberally and had to be taken to hospital within hours, hardly surprising as it was nail varnish! At least we didn't have the sergeant to contend with for the next 6–7 weeks and he was much mellower when he did return!

When at Dover a notice was put on HQ board inviting applications from soldiers to join the RAF as aircrew. As my brother had just joined up, I and another pal applied and we went to London for the initial interview, successfully passing we were told we would be sent for. A few weeks later a pal working in the orderly room told us a letter had been received asking for our transfer, but the reply had been sent back saying that as we were trained specialists in the Carrier Platoon on 'front line' duties in Dover, we could not be spared! I was later told by the RSM that I had 'marked my card' by showing eagerness to leave the regiment and this would not be forgotten!

Within days, however, I was given my second stripe with an extra few coppers a day! Plus extra responsibilities, including spells of acting as orderly sergeant, a very onerous time-consuming job, mounting of guards, overseeing mealtimes, attending when soldiers were 'put on charge' for disciplinary purposes. My promotion was not well received by some of the regular soldiers in the regiment! This caused me to get special attention when playing against them on the football field!

Enough rifles were now found to enable all of us to be so armed, goodbye to my Tommy gun, at least I could now join in properly with drills! Certainly it was much easier to keep clean for the weekly arms inspection when our 5 rounds of ammunition, later increased to 10, had to be produced. There was never any problem there as almost everyone had taken the opportunity when at Bisley on field firing to appropriate a few extra rounds! Except for the Tommy gun.

Our first army Christmas was memorable if only because our officers declined to carry out their usual function of serving Christmas dinner – saying that they were reluctant to do so as they knew what meat had been issued, but had also seen feathers around the cook house area – and pigs didn't have feathers! Especially as a complaint had been received from the nearby Cricketers Inn saying that there had been marked decrease in the number of ducks on their pond! Had they been required to serve poultry they would not have been able to report innocence in their reply to the complaint! At least the ducks went further with a few less mouths to feed!

We were now all hardened to cross channel shelling and being bombed by planes on their way back every night from London. We were frequently called out to go to crash sites and guard wreckage until the specialist RAF crash teams arrived, but later we were pleased to be relieved of this job, ostensibly because it was interfering with our designated training routine. We were not sorry as it could be quite harrowing.

Early in 1941 we were moved to Patrixbourne – a 'peaceful' village near Canterbury where half a dozen of us married men took the opportunity of bringing our wives to stay in the village cottages, all with the intention of 'starting families', although none ever did. Certainly my wife was always too much on edge and did not conceive! This only lasted a few weeks and then it was back to Dover, wives back to homes! After a few weeks at Dover, we moved to Tankerton near Whitstable where training came to a complete stop for 6–7 weeks whilst we worked 15 hours a day erecting scaffolding defence works on the shore stretching along the entire coast, our bit being from Herne Bay to Sheppey. Very hard, dirty work, especially working all day in the mud flats around Whitstable. We did have occasional breaks helping on farms, mostly threshing corn which was even harder and dirtier than the scaffolding although we did get plenty of tea, cakes etc. and an occasional 1/– from the farmer!

During this time guard duties had to be carried out as usual, leave the beach a couple of hours early, clean up, polish boots etc. and mount guard until 6.00a.m. next day! It was when I was Guard Commander on one such guard that I had my first brush with the RSM (Regimental Sergeant Major).

The 12 man guard was called out early in the morning by the inspecting orderly officer. During this inspection he called for a rifle inspection, all rifles being unloaded, of course. Except that when he gave order to present and clear rifles the last action was to 'fire', all did, one being a live round, just missing the officer. As guard commander I was promptly put under arrest. Later that day I was instructed to appear before the Commanding officer, just leaving me time to find out that one of the guard had a very dirty rifle – one which it was very difficult to clean sufficiently to pass inspection and so he had borrowed his pal's for the guard mounting.

His pal was due to go on guard next day so had called round and brought the dirty rifle and taken his own. When before the CO I explained this, the RSM then said I had broken guard rules by allowing a soldier not on guard to enter the guard room, producing the Guard commanders orders to back up his charge. These were read out to the CO and when I was asked for my defence I pointed out that the wording of the orders actually stated that any member of the regiment was entitled to enter the guard room. Case dismissed, the RSM was told to rewrite the orders and submit them to the orderly room for checking before the next guard was mounted.

The offending member of the guard and his pal both got 14 days jankers and were lucky to get away with it. Although the armourer did condemn the dirty rifle and issue a replacement!

Obviously I was not the flavour of the month with the RSM and frequently got given unpopular jobs, including taking jankers, almost as bad as doing them.

Since I had joined up, possibly because I was a year or so older than most and was married, I had many times been approached by fellow squaddies when they had problems with getting leave passes when the family had illness, marriage problems and military ditto. And my skirmish with the RSM led to even more such approaches!!

A few weeks after the above events, I was given the job of taking a prisoner to a field punishment camp (prison) situated in a very isolated tented site near Hythe. The prisoner, a regular soldier with over 10 years service and well known as a trouble maker, had escaped when being taken to the same prison a few weeks earlier, so I was given a further soldier to escort him. All equipment had to be taken by the two of us; our rifles and full equipment, the prisoner likewise, plus 4 blankets, kit bag and palliasse. Obviously it was too much for him to carry so on the 3 mile trek from station to the prison, we each carried some of his kit. On approaching the barbed wire surrounding the compound there was a loud shout from a prison sergeant, 'Who's the bloody prisoner! Double march!!' We had to hand his kit back to the prisoner, marking double time whilst handing over papers and the prisoner was taken off our hands, ultimately being sent on our way, 'double time out of sight – and think yourself bloody lucky I'm not keeping you here as well!' parting message from the sergeant!

I met the prisoner some 4 months later when he told me the 12 weeks he had spent there were the worst in all his army life and there was no way he was ever going to transgress in future. Almost the entire time was spent scrubbing duckboards and edging stones, then whitewashing them only for the camp sergeant to accidentally slip off the boards so making them muddy again. Repeat the process!!!

A lot of wives (including Glad) joined us at Whitstable and so we were able to enjoy each other's company during the long periods we were away on duty and exercises! Not forgetting the various 'spoils of war' – apples, pears, potatoes (sometimes a chicken!) which carrier drivers collected, they being quite satisfied with a share of resultant pies, tarts stews etc. Again we were able to visit the local cinema at reduced prices once a week and it was on such an outing we had one of the closest shaves during our time in Kent. We were used to the noise of German planes going over on their nightly raids on London and hearing exploding bombs being dropped nearby when they couldn't drop them on their intended London targets. Halfway through the film we heard one bomb dropping, then another much closer, this causing the roof to fall on us including many tons of mud!

In pitch darkness we scrambled out with fortunately only a few cuts and broken arms (not ours). We were both OK and made our way back the couple of miles to Tankerton having to shelter with dozens of others beneath a railway bridge when another string of bombs dropped. Next day, we realised how lucky we had been when we learnt that 9 or 10 people (including 2 of our regimental pals) had been killed and dozens injured when a bomb had hit a queue outside a fish and chip shop only 100 yards from the cinema. Although Glad complained that her special treat nylons (or similar) had been ruined!

Fortunately we were never called upon to do any real

soldiering! Probably just as well as we were all very raw – possibly 'cometh the day – cometh the man' but luckily we did not have to find out!

Whilst at Whitstable, I was sent on a three week PTI (physical training instructor) course at the central army gymnasium at Aldershot where all the tutors were sports stars from every sphere, football, cricket, boxing, swimming. In charge of my squad of 20 or so was a British olympic diving champion. (I think his name was Mather). The soldier I palled up with was a professional footballer – a lovely chap who it was difficult to get to enlarge on that fact except that on the third day, we were given football instruction. When the instructor asked if anyone present played football, he stepped forward whereupon the instructor showed us how to trap the ball etc. and asked him to do likewise. As it was obvious he didn't need any instruction Mather asked him what experience he had to be advised he had captained Wolverhampton Wanderers FC in the last cup final before the war. Further 'clangers' dropped by the instructor: he called for boxing volunteers and got one who was ruling Canadian army middleweight champion; another long jump, 1936 olympic finalist! and several others.

Returning to my unit, I had to take early morning PT parades of 4 platoons at 5.30a.m., 6.00a.m., 6.30a.m. and 7.00a.m. after which return to my platoon and carry out full normal duties! These included numerous 24 hour exercises but one 3 week effort which is worth mentioning. We were to be the Germans, having landed on the Norfolk coast and moving towards London. To start we had to make a rapid journey through London to Epping Forest. The battalion were moved in convoys of trucks, the carriers and 20 or so motor cyclists in a separate echelon. 5 echelons of trucks and our group were each escorted by 3 police motor cyclists. They travelled in front of each echelon, one staying immediately in front, two speeding off, one stopping ordinary traffic when we approached major roads, leap-frogging to ensure that we maintained a good steady speed. This worked out OK for the trucks, however when going down a hill approaching the Old Kent Road the escort had not been able to stop traffic to ensure we had a clear road so he merely gave the halt signal with upstretched hand and stopped.

As he was only about 30 yards clear of the first carrier which required 50–60 yards to stop he received a light bump from that carrier. The next carrier hit one in front with slightly heavier bump and so on. I came round the corner at 30–35 miles an hour (the last carrier was always going faster than those in front in order to keep up) to find carriers all over the road. I crashed into the carnage with following motorcycles crashing into my carrier. Followed a hectic half hour sorting things out, the only real damage was to two motorcycles, virtual scrap once wheels etc had been cannibalised to keep other bikes serviceable.

We proceeded on our way until when crossing London bridge my carrier stripped a bogey wheel, one of the wheels which supported the track, where a 12" length of rubber some 2" thick had peeled off. It was impossible to proceed so we pulled into a side street just over the bridge, sending one of the bikes to catch the LAD (light aid detachment) lorry carrying spares and report to our officer. We proceeded to take off the track and broken Bogey, quickly attracting a large audience eventually some couple of hundred strong, one of whom offered cigarettes quickly followed by gifts of cakes, tea, drinks, biscuits and then passing around a hat when nearly £10 was given to us! The LAD lorry arrived, also our officer who accused us of causing the damage with a screwdriver! Not true on this occasion but he departed after giving me the map reference in Epping forest and warning us, 'and don't go near Joe Crow's place,' this being my driver's home at Stratford, East London. We started on our way but within a couple of miles it was too dark to proceed – we had no lights at the front, merely a light shining onto a white circle painted on the axle beneath the carrier to warn following traffic. Luckily we were only ½ mile from Joe's place so where better to park up! We were entertained at his local, had a few hours 'kip' on the floor in the front room, up at 5.00a.m. arriving at map reference at 7.00a.m. just in time for a shave and breakfast! The officer accepted our reason for not arriving earlier – no mention of Joe's place – or how we managed to drive in the dark in the morning but not at night!

After sharing out our 'spoils of misadventure' – nearly £1 to each carrier plus a few chocolates, sweets and cigarettes (out of sight of the officer of course), we were on the move again and after spending a few days of hide and seek with our direct opposition, the allies Canadian first division, one morning found us near Eye in Suffolk. Our carriers were camouflaged in a hedge on a short straight single track country road. As No. 10 carrier I was at the rear, the first one which the approaching allied forces would encounter. Backed into a hedge a few yards from a corner approaching the straight road behind us we covered with our Bren Gun a 350 yard open stretch of road down which our opposition would come, which they did. Opening fire with blanks, causing them to dive to whatever cover they could find, we then started up and drove around the corner when they formed up again. Travelling at about 25–30 miles an hour we found a roadman laden with usual shovel, pickaxe and broom casually wheeling his pushbike down the centre of the road! The grass on both sides was quite high so our driver just pulled onto the verge to pass him, except that the verge was only about a foot wide sloping away to a ditch with running water, hence the growth of grass. Next minute we found ourselves upside down in the ditch, fortunately with the carrier, upside down, resting on banks on either side and so not injuring us! We quickly crawled out fearing that the carrier would catch fire. It didn't but we were immediately captured by the allies! With labels tied around our necks we salvaged our belongings from the carrier and were marched off to their rear and put in a 'POW' compound where we spent next 48 hours by which time us Germans had been pushed back towards the North Sea.

Now restricted to living on our own issue iron rations, hard biscuits, bully beef, condensed milk and tinned jam, we really missed the extras we had been able to get when on the move in the carrier. It was even difficult to get access to boiling water to make tea, and cocoa made with cold water is not very appetising! Fortunately after 3 days of captivity we were released, our 'POW' labels marked with the time and day of release and told to rejoin our units. We hadn't a clue where they were so tongue in cheek assumed that they meant our base back in Kent.

Three motorcycle combinations from our platoon had also been captured so we did a little juggling of personnel, Londoners on two and two plus myself who lived in Bristol in the other we started on our way back to Kent – except we seemed to have taken the wrong turn somewhere and found ourselves in Bristol – hardly the shortest way from Suffolk to Kent! Knowing the exercise was not due to finish for another 6–7 days we spent 5 days at home then made our way back to Kent where we arrived a few hours before the battalion!

We had no difficulty in scrounging petrol for the journey, we only had to show our 'POW' labels and both petrol and invitations to feed at their cookhouses were readily forthcoming. Likewise, reporting back to our platoon officer we somehow discovered we had 'lost' our labels and so there was no way anyone could check when we were released! And, of course, we had no idea where the other chaps taken 'prisoner' were – they arrived 2 days after we got back!

Shortly after the above episode I was called into the battalion HQ one afternoon – where the RSM gloatingly told me, 'You tried to leave this unit before, well now you are leaving, catch the 6.00p.m. train to London en route to join the second battalion in Yorkshire.' Adding 'that is a regular unit – let's see how well your stripes go down with them'. Leaving Glad to make her own way back to Bristol via London, I was joined on the journey by a sergeant from the motor transport platoon but not for long as, within hours of joining the second battalion at Boroughbridge, he was on his way back again under escort! Apparently the move was so quick he had been unable to take any steps to cover up certain irregularities which had immediately come to light – like hundreds of gallons of petrol, dozens of tyres, numerous spares etc which could not be accounted for. I never did hear what happened to him!

I soon knew I was in a regular unit, reporting first to the RSM, then the adjutant and finally the second in command. Their immediate response after checking my papers was, 'Two tapes with your length of service – we shall have to see about that!' Although I was supposedly transferred as a specialist carrier corporal I was immediately posted to a rifle company, totally new to me. A week or so later with another corporal also just arrived from the fourth battalion and 20 others from the Seconds we found ourselves sent on a NCO cadre, a 2 week course where they sorted out the wheat from the chaff at the end of which we came out first and second of the 22 and were immediately transferred to another company in the regiment where there were no vacancies for sergeants. 7 of those who were way behind us in the Cadre were transferred the other way and were soon sporting 3 tapes, all regular soldiers of course!

Days later I was given the task of taking a party of 30 or so to Dishforth aerodrome, there to go through the gas chambers. During the 8 mile march, I found out I was the only one who had not had 7 days embarkation leave. On reaching our Nissan hut quarters after the 8 mile march back I was accosted by the RSM who asked what I was doing still 'hanging around'.

It appeared that the adjutant had just discovered I had not had any embarkation leave and had put me on 48 hours leave starting at noon that day, about 5 hours before I had got back from the gas chambers. This test was supposed to give you confidence in the efficiency of your gas mask – you put it on, spent half an hour marking time and on similar exercises in the room then took it off before being let out into the fresh air coughing and spluttering a few minutes later!

The RSM said not to worry, a truck would take me and several others to York station to catch the 8.00a.m. train to London the next morning, telling me to get my train ticket and pass from the quartermaster when evening dinner at the NCO mess was over at about 9.30p.m. Not being too happy with this I collared the QM in his quarters and he went with me to his office where I was given the ticket and told I had to take *all* my kit on leave with me just in case – 'Home' and 'Tropical'. Lugging 2 kit bags, all my kit and rifle, I decided to try and hitch hike. Within minutes of reaching the Great North Road running past the camp, I was picked up in a car. After hearing my story, the driver, who was only going to Harrogate, decided to take me all the way to Leeds station where I caught the 10.00p.m. train to Bristol. Joining the train I must have gone straight to sleep, waking up at 6.30a.m. next morning in Bristol Temple Meads station, thankfully the end of the journey for that train! I had about 24 hours at home then back to Boroughbridge to find immediate plans to send us abroad had been changed!

Back to training, including a day long field firing course on a farm near Richmond where once again I nearly met a sticky end! Using live ammunition, I was leading one section down a shallow, winding river bed with other sections one on each bank alongside. Rounding a bend a 'target' sprang up about 5 yards ahead, at the same time one of the flanking sections also saw the target and tossed a live no. 36 hand grenade, which hit the target and bounced back towards me. I let off a round and then hurled myself backwards causing complete mayhem, guns going off everywhere. Miraculously no one was injured although some of us were soaked and covered in mud! On returning to our unit we were all quizzed as to who shot a cow that day. Nothing to do with us except that everyone was docked 1/6d each barrack room damages – although we didn't have beef on the menu during the next few weeks!! We were later to find out that the officers mess did enjoy roast beef, beef steaks and stews for weeks!

Loaded onto lorries at 4.00a.m. one morning with all our kit we thought, 'This is it'. During the 7–8 hours journey we only stopped once to have a brief meal and attend to needs of nature! This latter had been a matter of considerable concern from the time we first embussed, resulting in us cutting cards to decide whose mess tin should be used to enable us to relieve ourselves. Fortunately it didn't turn out to be mine! Eventually to our relief we found ourselves NOT at Liverpool but in Banbury, Oxon, billeted in a loft over the stables behind a public house with a wooden floor with huge gaps above hay filled stables below! There was a terrible risk of fire, with only 20" wide stone steps to exit. It was possibly good training, certainly no one was ever allowed to light up! As no lighting was allowed, we were completely in the dark during the night, which resulted in several bad accidents when using the steps.

Being recognised as a good map reader I was given the job of taking some 30 men out on a battalion exercise. Leaving at 4.00a.m. in the dark we marched 5 miles or so to the designated point in the middle of a raging blizzard.

Our orders were to deploy in hedges etc. around the map reference point, camouflaging and only revealing ourselves if and when the battalion had passed through without seeing us. We had to make huge detours so as not to leave tracks in the snow but after lying in freezing snow all day without seeing anyone I called off the exercise and we marched back to Banbury. Reporting to the RSM I was told I must have gone to the wrong reference point. Joined by the adjutant, next day we drove to where we had been, both RSM and Adjutant agreed we were in the correct place, we were told that the officer leading the battalion had taken them to a point several miles away. That officer was not seen again, certainly he did not go to India with us later. Neither did another officer who made a real hash of his orders during Adjutants parade a few weeks later.

Parading 4 rifle companies, each of about 120 men on a local football field flanked with hundreds of 40 gallon barrels, he lost all control when giving orders, 'advance in column', 'advance in line' etc. – resulting in all the chaps having the time of their lives climbing over barrels stacked 4 and 5 high etc. They were being keen to embarrass that particular officer!

On another occasion we travelled for a live ammunition training stint on the Severn Estuary near Severn Beach. The battalion was deployed on the south side of the river with a detachment sent upwind to release gas filled balloons for us to fire at. Unfortunately there was no wind and the balloons didn't co-operate. So beating parties were sent out to raise whatever birds they could. There ensued the most spectacular show, a small sparrow would be the object of a couple of dozen Bren guns and hundreds of rifles all firing tracer bullets. Several hours of great fun, not for the birds though, but I don't think any were shot down! At the end of the day, by pure coincidence I found myself in a lorry which got lost, finding myself with a dozen other chaps (including an officer) who all lived in Bristol! So we decided to visit our homes, being picked up on a strict rota system which I had to arrange, arriving back at Banbury just before reveille next morning!

When embarkation became imminent once again many of us brought our wives to stay at Banbury.

Again I clicked for a nasty job, being called one very bad night during a heavy snowstorm to guard a bomber which had crashed when trying to take off at Edge Hill aerodrome. Our orders were to deploy around the crash site, fanning out at first light and collecting all debris (including body parts) into a single defined area. It was a very unpleasant job, particularly when a gauntlet glove was found which was found to be already occupied when the finder tried to put it on! We were very pleased when we were relieved by an RAF unit. A few days before we were due to embark one of our corporals was caught stealing rations from the cook house for his girl friend.

Although – or possibly because – the RSM knew my wife was in Banbury, I was given the job of escorting him and keeping him under close arrest, handing him over to the HQ guard at 10.00p.m. and collecting him again at 8.00a.m.

This meant taking him to the pictures, to pubs, canteen and walks with my wife, not easy as I was not allowed to use handcuffs! This was all very exhausting until the last night when I got permission to turn him over to the guardhouse at 6.00p.m. He was then the responsibility of the guard to take him down to the station and hand him over to me again before the train left at 6.00a.m.

I slept through the alarm set for 4.00a.m., waking at nearly 5.00 and rushed off without really saying goodbye to Glad, putting on my uniform whilst running the 2 miles to the billet. Too late, I met my platoon, in the pitch dark marching down to the station. I cannot tell of my relief when told by my platoon mates, 'It's all right corporal – we've got your kit.' And they did – having shared it out amongst themselves and someone answering my name when roll call was made. As it was so dark I fell in, my kit being passed to me and our officer never knew.

We took over escort duty again, and eventually found ourselves in Liverpool where on embarking on the 'luxury' liner *Reino Del Pacifico* I was told by the Redcap officer of the army police guarding the gangway to release the prisoner as all charges would automatically be dropped once on board. I was to learn many years later that when the battalion went to Japan on occupation duties in 1946 – this 'Lance Corporal' was then RSM!!

On embarking one of my platoon, our Jewish tailor, went straight over to the other side and was seasick although there was no water in sight, the ship being stuck high and dry on a sea of mud! With a peacetime crew of 600/700 carrying less than one thousand passengers this 17,000 ton ship had been hastily converted into a troopship and was now carrying more than 8,000 troops plus over 1,000 crew. The conversion mainly consisted of most of the holds being fitted out with long 20" wide mess tables with 12" wide bench seats on either side and a gap of about 9" between opposite seats from each side of the hull to a 24" passage in the centre. Set above the tables were hooks to accept hammocks, only enough hammocks for just over half the troops, however, the remainder had to sleep on tables, under tables etc. anywhere they could find. There were two large tubes running down through our deck from that above and as one was right at the end of our table I laid claim to a bed space with my head on my lifejacket pillow against the tube. During the night, when the tide turned, the ship pulled over into midstream frightening us all to death and we then found out that the tubes housed the anchor chains hence the noise when the anchor was dropped was really horrendous! We all thought we had been bombed! Facilities were primitive to say the least. Whole decks had been converted to toilets, long galvanised troughs raised above deck level so that one end sloped out through a porthole. A long row of toilet 'seats' were arranged back to back, to reach them one had to step up a couple of full length plank steps and then be seated with occupants of adjoining seat back to back with those on next row! With permanently running sea water constantly flushing through the porthole! The stench arising with some 300/400 men at a time using these toilets took us weeks to come to terms with, particularly as for the first 3 days at sea all hatches were closed whilst we all had diarrhoea and sea sickness. Imagine the scenes – one would be meeting the need of nature one minute, turning round and being sea sick the next. One minute you would be talking to a face 3ft or 4ft away, next minute facing ***** at half that distance hoping there would be no involuntary response!! I couldn't think of how to explain the position more delicately!

Within 24 hours of sailing it was announced over the tannoy that because of a logistical miscalculation fresh water supplies were totally insufficient. As a consequence everyone would be rationed to half a mug of fresh water every day! This had to be drawn every morning and we grouped ourselves into gangs to make it stretch as far as possible.

This meant using a quarter of a mug of water for 5 or 6 to clean teeth, then shave, finally washing – using a flannel for this purpose, finishing off with a salt water shower, although we quickly found out that using issued salt water soap and salt water soon dried up our skin. Using the above system, we could then keep and at least store some fresh water for drinking – and freshening up our mouths after being sick!

When eventually we were allowed up on deck we all tried to find deck space where we could sleep, a number of us managed to locate space beneath the anchor chain, rigging up ground sheets (strictly against orders) to give a degree of shelter from rain and sea spray. We had to take it in turns to 'guard' our chosen bed space!

We had several regular old soldiers on our deck and they were very much pressed into service during the first 7/10 days whilst the rest of us were getting our sea legs! The food was terrible even if we had been in fit state to eat it! Only the morning porridge and plain bread and cheese for supper could be faced by most of us as the main meal of potatoes, bully beef, soya link sausages with variety of vegetables were made virtually inedible during cooking. Potatoes were tipped direct from sacks into the huge boilers, no attempt to wash or throw out the rotten ones and certainly not peel them. Although there would have been no lack of volunteers had we been asked to peel them, as this may have led to any such volunteers being able to scrounge an extra mug of tea from the galley whilst helping to offset our boredom. Even the tea and occasional cocoa were made with half (or quarter) fresh water topped up with sea water making the 'tea' almost black but even so very acceptable.

The NCO in charge of each mess table was issued with plastic tokens for each meal – one for porridge, one for the main dish, one for tea and one for sweet. Men detailed to collect meals had to hand in a token when they collected the food and once a token was surrendered there was no way of getting further rations!

There was no more food even if rations tipped up onto the always slippery gangways, as frequently happened, particularly with the large shallow dishes requiring two hands to hold whereas one hand was really required to hang onto hand rails when ship rolled. This led to some most unhygienic acts, food scooped up from the filthy deck and as we were informed by several of the mess orderlies after we had landed, on numerous occasions when porridge was being carried a sudden 'roll' had caused the orderly to be sick into the porridge. With no chance of getting a further supply of this most popular dish the only answer was to stir it in and carry on to the mess deck. Probably improved the flavour! Which also happened when rice was on the menu and as with porridge who would ever notice! Many of the men virtually lived up on the open deck coming down only to use the 'toilet' relying on their mates to take them up food and drink. Amongst these was the aforementioned Barney who was seasick for the entire 6 weeks of the voyage. I took him up a couple of slices of bread on one occasion and found him as usual leaning over the ship's side. Accosting him, just as I handed over the bread the ship gave a big roll and I was sick over both the bread and our hands! More food for the fish! Not that they or I heard Barney's words of thanks!

When we boarded the ship, all rifles and our tropical kit were handed into the armoury and nearby storage holds. One of the old soldiers told a few of us to put some of our tropical kit, shorts and light shirts etc. into our other kit bag as we wouldn't be able to get at them until we landed and the weather would certainly hot up. We were grateful for this once we had passed over the equator, in fact, wearing these shorts made us feel overdressed, all the other chaps simply wearing Blighty underpants!

For some reason of all the troops on board only our battalion kept up any pretence of military 'correctness', daily orders being published detailing a full days training for all ranks. Every platoon was allocated deck space and had to undertake lectures for 5/6 hours a day. This was OK for things like map reading, first aid, gas lectures, regimental history (a big must with our unit), but drills and other training were also included.

Gas lectures were a great bore although we were somewhat relieved when on the very first lecture the 'specialist' sergeant giving it was asked a question after some 5 minutes and we then realised he had memorised the whole lecture parrot fashion. He had to start from scratch if interrupted he never succeeded in completing the lecture, although it was given almost daily for the entire voyage!!

Rifle drill was a regular drill every day without rifles, going through all the motions with the NCO having to correct them. 'So & So too late, get in order' 'Raise your elbow more', 'Keep in step' etc. etc.

All rifles having been handed in, it took rather a lot of imagination to carry out such tasks! There was always a large number of men from other units watching, laughing their heads off and proffering very crude advice.

A particular favourite (with the audience, anyway) was target snap shooting. The platoon paraded alongside the ship's rail. One man was sent forward, on a given signal he released imaginary balloons – as these imaginary balloons passed the line of men they had to shoot them down with imaginary rifles! With the NCOs correcting their holding of the 'rifle', telling them not to snatch at the trigger, stop shooting once the 'balloon' had gone past as this could endanger men further down the line etc. And we were all grown men! After one such drill on 'E' deck aft, the top deck right at the back of the ship, my platoon's next parade was a kit inspection on our mess deck 'A'-1 forward, right down below at the front of ship. I led off with 30 men following only to find our way blocked by another platoon every few yards, retracing our steps and finding an alternative route we finished up by going round the upper gangway in the engine room and getting a right telling off by the engine room staff. On arrival at our mess deck where our officer was waiting my platoon of 30 had dwindled to 8, all the rest had sloped off saying later that they had lost their way. No excuse for me though, the officer put me on a charge to appear before the Battalion commander, 'Inefficiency in leading my platoon in the field.' Duly appearing before the CO, a real professional regular officer and a very much respected officer, I stated my case – what had happened, the lack of forethought in the timing of the two parades and the fact that 8 of the men who had 'lost their way' were Battalion boxers, good soldiers, but not the easiest of men to control. Result, case dismissed and my officer told to stay behind after I was dismissed. I never found out what happened then, suffice to say that I was later given every rough job that arose!

Every day there was a ceremonial guard mounting of about 80 men and NCO! This took place on an open deck liberally dotted with air ventilators, iron bollards for tying up ropes, chains and the like.

Again without rifles we had to act exactly as if armed and on the barrack square – line up and right dress, spacing yourself in line with the next man, who would frequently be an air ventilator. Marching in time, stepping (often tripping) over ropes and chains and obeying all orders given by a tap of the drum! This always provided welcome entertainment for several thousand men all offering their usual advice!

Despite all the time taken up with this 'training', time went by very slowly, largely taken up by playing cards, housey housey (bingo) and when dark, singing led by a chap with an accordion. Reading was also popular although there were never enough salacious books to go around!

The accordion player decided to raffle the instrument when nearing the end of the voyage, selling tickets at 6d each. Invariably when approached to buy a ticket the seller was asked, what the hell would I do with an accordion, I can't play, being given the answer if you win I will buy it back for £50. Having sold over £800 worth of tickets he duly bought the accordion back!

After a short stop (no shore leave) putting on fresh supplies, water etc. at Freetown a further 2 weeks was spent on huge detour across the Atlantic then back to Capetown where we were put ashore and bussed to a splendid tented camp near Pietermaritzberg some 20 miles away. Enjoying the best food we ever had during our army service we were made to pay for this by undertaking very heavy intensive training, including route marches up the inland side of Table Mountain. During the voyage, we had all had to wear plimsolls (daps or sandshoes) and army boots were not allowed. Once ashore it was the reverse, we had to wear boots all the time including when asleep to 'harden our feet!'

Whilst in this camp 3 or 4 men absconded and to the best of our knowledge were never found! Returning to the ship, we were given shore leave for two days, finding apartheid, the black and white rules, particularly in pubs very hard to accept. We all took the opportunity of sending gifts home leaving this to the shops to arrange and had no reports of any not being received by our families.

On our way again this time we had to call in at Durban to put ashore a dangerously ill soldier then on to Bombay. At this time we were told our ship had originally been intended to go to Madagascar, but a single British Brigade had taken the island a few days earlier so once again fate had smiled on us!

On our arrival at Bombay our platoon officer was put in charge of the baggage party, transferring all the battalion kit and supplies from the ship to a goods train en-route to Poona. Obviously, I received the sticky end of this, being put in charge of loading onto the train. These were all closed goods trucks, the work was very hard and also very hot. We finished early next morning and here my memory is NIL.

Six of us were taken straight to hospital at arrival at Poona, all suffering from heat stroke with temperatures in the 105–106 area. The major symptom is the total inability to sweat, the treatment, total immersion in ice cold water, constantly replenished with ice, with 2/3 nurses engaged in spooning water over our bodies to prevent our temperatures from rising even further. It must have worked because 3 days later I awoke to find my temperature considerably reduced but I was suffering from pneumonia, apparently the only alternative to death!

A further 10/12 days saw me over this, and I was put into a tented convalescent camp, still on a very restricted diet, milk drinks, jellies and other soft foods. When finally allowed out of our tents, three of us ventured into a nearby canteen where we simply couldn't resist the temptation posed by the tantalising smell of a fried egg butty liberally smothered in sauce! Very satisfying, except 3 or 4 hours later found us actually rolling on the floor in agony. The doctor was called, found out what we had done and walked away saying, 'Serve them right' but in more specific language!

One end of our large tented ward had been sheeted off and was being used as a VD clinic. From our very first week in the army, we had regularly been visited by our medical officer, a captain whose peacetime practice was at Weston-Super-Mare, and were given lectures on venereal disease and its consequences. These continued weekly whilst on the ship and he always prefaced his lecture, and finished it, by telling us 'If you catch VD and then tell me you must have caught it off the lavatory seat I shall only comment that's a funny place to take women.' (or words to that effect). Certainly I and the vast majority of my fellow soldiers were never tempted to stray even after nearly 4 years abroad. This was reinforced in my case by hearing 'sympathetic treatment' given out to men visiting the VD clinic in our tent at Poona!

When I was sufficiently recovered in hospital at Poona, I wrote 5 or 6 letters to Glad, suitably date spaced, telling numerous lies but no mention of my illness. Mail took anything from 6 to 10 weeks to arrive and some 2 months later

I received several letters from Glad which had been chasing me around India expressing considerable concern as she had received a telegram telling her I was dangerously ill with NYD (Not Yet Diagnosed) fever. All my efforts to hide my illness had been in vain. Rather surprisingly, she had only received the one telegram but had never been advised of my recovery and that I was back in my unit!

Five weeks after going to hospital with heat stroke, I rejoined my unit, where I was promptly put on 'Attend B' (excused duties) for 14 days and equally promptly was made orderly sergeant for the whole battalion. This was really hard work, being on the go from 5.30a.m., getting the cookhouse staff up and on duty, supervising all meals, overseeing sick parade, jankers, mounting guards and checking return at midnight of men returning from day passes. I would go to bed about 12.30a.m., get up at 5.30a.m.! And this was supposed to be hastening my convalescence! It was a relief to return to full duties, although far from light.

Training was very heavy, route marches most days and being stationed at Juhu beach – our camp – was on the beach beneath tall palm trees with a river on the land side of our camp – thus within yards of starting on our marches we had to walk through the river and were wet through from the waist down. We didn't mind the wet clothes, but wet socks and boots at the start of a 18–25 mile march was anything but welcome. Being so unfit, I was constantly left trailing behind my platoon sometimes coming in half an hour after them and being duly reprimanded by our officer. Yes, the same one as on the ship!

Visits to the regimental medical officer were met with equal lack of sympathy and understanding. Our regimental second in command, the ex-Olympic steeplechaser mentioned earlier,

71

had set up an assault course on the beach. This consisted of ropes tied to the bottom of one tree and the top of another approx 50ft tall then across at high level to another, a further rope sagging to halfway down another, finishing with a three foot water trench about 50 yards long dug into the bank of the river. The bottom of the trench was always filled with 12"/18" of water with rolls of Dannert barbed wire pressed down into the trench. After traversing the ropes, or after failing to complete them, all were required to crawl through the trench, on our backs, holding a rifle between our knees. Once again I nearly 'had my chips', apparently passing out and nearly drowning, my plight being noticed by the soldier following me. I woke up many hours later in the main Bombay Civilian Hospital ending up with pneumonia once again.

There was only a 3 week spell before returning to my unit again and resuming full training. At least I didn't break any arms or legs as did some 20/25 of my pals when falling off the ropes! Even sand is not soft when you fall 40 or 50 feet!

On one of the exercises, we boarded a small ship at Bombay and were put ashore at about 3.00a.m. on a beach with orders to proceed inland from this spur of land approx. 8 miles to a beach on the far side. We were timed to arrive at first light then to make a bayonet charge to repel troops being put ashore by landing craft. We had to assist a troop of Royal artillery, helping them to pull a 25 pounder gun. To make our deadline meant running most of the way. We arrived on time, made our bayonet charge and thoroughly exhausted, lay down until the chuck wagon arrived with a plentiful supply of corned beef stew and mugs of tea. We had nearly finished our meal when the aforesaid second in command arrived on his horse, congratulated us on our efforts and finishing by saying, 'You can have the rest of the day off once you have

Bombay leave, 1944. Ronnie Mann and author.

rejoined your ship.' It was 8 miles away on the other side of the headland!!

There followed further deployments to Secunderabad and Ahmednagar, where we carried on training plus some security jobs, these requiring us to get up at 3.00a.m. or 4.00a.m., travel in darkness to surround local villages and stop anyone from leaving. At dawn the Indian security units went in and arrested known suspects. It was a most revealing duty as just before dawn, the villagers, men, women and children came out to attend to the needs of nature without knowing we were there!

Then we were posted back to Juhu beach for a spell when, providing you could prove that you could swim, the test being a 200 course between two posts set in the sea, wearing full kit including boots and carrying rifle, the reward was a half day pass once a week to Bombay and a free pass to a big open air swimming pool.

When stationed at Secunderabad I took part in what can only be described as a criminal act – or at least being party to one! A number of chaps in my platoon had been ripped off when buying films, paying over twice as much in a shop in the bazaar as the price charged for exactly the same film at a nearby shop. They tried to get their money refunded without success.

Another of our platoon mates, a Londoner called Scotty, persuaded a dozen or so of us to join him in 'screwing' the said camera shop owner. It was a very small shop, possibly about 8ft × 5ft, with a display of cameras in the window. We all crowded into the shop, no room to move, all clamouring for attention.

Whilst this was going on, Scotty helped himself to a quite expensive camera from the window, we let him move to the counter where he told the owner he wanted to sell it. He was offered a price of about 50 rupees (15 to the £1.00), Scotty then remonstrated with the owner saying he had an identical camera in the window for 600 rupees. Eventually he 'sold' the camera to its legal owner for 110 rupees! The shop keeper couldn't come after us when he found out, there were too many soldiers still in the shop. Very few shops had doors, they were merely stalls, all the stock being taken home at the end of the day.

During this time I had to go before a medical board in Bombay after which I was told I had only one effective lung and would have to leave the unit. I was also further informed that it was being recommended that I was sent to South Africa for a period of rehabilitation prior to returning to England. When I asked for further clarification, I was told that once back in England I would be found suitable sedentary occupation.

I had never heard this word before. On being told it meant light work done without any outlay of physical effort, sitting down all day, and as long as I didn't attempt any physical job I should be all right for a good many years. I nearly got into trouble by virtually shouting, 'I came out here a very fit man, a physical training instructor and I would rather not go back if it means spending the rest of my life an invalid.' No reaction from the medical officer when he saw this report, I was merely told to rejoin my normal duties. I was continually falling out on marches, I simply did not have the energy to keep up, especially when we were sent on further combined operations training at the lakes about 20 miles from Bombay which supplied all the drinking water for Bombay and the surrounding area.

We were camped in a very flat barren area with no villages

within miles and unbearably hot and humid.

There was a chronic shortage of water although a huge pipeline ran right through the camp, a steel pipe about 72" diameter which carried the water to Bombay. One night there was an unfortunate accident – a .55 rifle was fired in error right through the top of the pipe resulting in a huge stream of water shooting 50 feet or so into the air on each side. We couldn't let all this water go to waste so quickly scrounging suitable containers and cutting tops off 40 gallon drums we provided ample fresh water for the whole battalion both for drinking and very welcome shower/baths! The same day as we learnt the site was deemed uninhabitable, hence no Indians lived there, I was told to report to the medical officer who I later suspected had been drinking, to be told (his actual words!) 'The battle for the saving of your soul has been lost and you are being posted to Deolali in the morning.'

It was only then that I realised he had never given me any examinations or tests, pulse, blood, heart (with stethoscope etc.) since arriving in India and certainly had had no reason to do so before leaving England!

Presumably he had relied entirely on the medical records which always had to be handed in whenever I rejoined the regiment from hospital. In view of the huge numbers reporting sick daily mostly with 'tropical' illnesses, he had little time to do more than categorise his patients: Attend 'A' – Back to full duties and report sick in 4–5 days; Attend 'B' – excused full duties, light duty only, no marching, exercises, guard duties, report to orderly sergeant then duties in cook house (peeling spuds etc.) or in quartermaster's stores. (Unless you were a corporal – then you were almost inevitably made orderly sergeant working an 18 hour day!); Attend 'C' – very rarely given, as it meant take to your bed and await a visit from the medical officer unless there was a spare bed in the battalion sick tent!

I always had great respect and admiration for this medical officer and this was certainly re-inforced by troops in the field where he established a great rapport with the many hundreds of casualties later encountered in the Battle of Kohima and subsequently through Burma from Mandalay to Rangoon when he was affectionately known as 'Joe' to all and sundry.

His last words to me were to pick up my sealed medical records from his sergeant on the way out!

I was sent with about 10 other privates by truck the next day to Deolali which was a huge base re-enforcement camp sited in a pretty terrible situation, not dissimilar to the one we had just left. In fact, a long stay at this place would send one round the bend hence the well known saying – in the army anyway – of describing anyone acting at all strangely of having 'Deolali Tap'!

Duly posted to the camp HQ staff, as were all arrivals sent there from India based regiments, I was immediately made semi-permanent orderly sergeant with the usual onerous duties.

All re-inforcing troops arriving from UK except complete units, regiments brigades etc., were routed through Deolali prior to being sent on to units already in India. One of my tasks was allocating duties to HQ men, including dining hall jobs, dishing out meals under supervision of other NCOs whose main duty was to make sure no one came back for unauthorised seconds. One such NCO was a regular soldier who had joined up in 1930, had not been home since and had been evacuated from Rangoon a few weeks before Burma was overrun by the Japs.

He came to me asking to be relieved of his job so that he could spend time with his younger brother who had just

77

arrived from the UK and had recognised him from photographs sent home during peacetime. When the NCO had left the UK his younger brother was only 7 years old and the NCO had never seen a photograph of him except when he was only 9 years old!

All new men from units already in India, mostly medically graded as myself, were given intelligence tests. This was the first time I had come across them, a three hour written test including allocating 'square diagrams into square holes' etc. This was to try and ensure what abilities off the parade ground could be used to the best advantage and the results ensured men could be posted to non front-line units where they could be used to advantage. No one was ever told how they had been rated. I saw all my pals gradually being posted away but no news of a posting for me. There were several untoward incidents whilst I was at Deolali. When leaving the Dorsets, I was given a sealed envelope which contained all our records which had to be handed over to HQ at Deolali – to be held in orderly room tent.

A miniature whirlwind swept through the camp one day sending the tent and belongings high into the air, a single path about 20 yards wide was scythed through the camp including the orderly room. There followed a huge scramble to collect one's kit (fortunately NOT including mine). Also picked up were hundreds of service records.

Most were handed in but not until the finder had tried, and frequently succeeded in locating the owner of same, when he would be given the opportunity of reading them and getting rid of any that were unfavourable! I was certainly shown mine, but my only concern was that they should be returned intact!

When at Deolali I realised how fortunate (in a peculiar way) I had been in joining the Dorsets and NOT a Welsh unit where there were so many 'Jones', 'Williams' and 'Davies' etc., that they were all identified by last 3 numbers of their army number – 760 Jones, 102 Williams – I would have been 281 Davis!!!

The ever changing population of Deolali camp was around 7,000–8,000 including a large number of East Africans all in regiments officered by British officers. These very big men – almost all were well over 6ft tall – were very respectful of all white soldiers and always saluted all white NCOs although not supposed to. The village of Deolali a few miles away was out of bounds to all British troops, but this did not apply to the Africans.

Every day I had to send out what came to be called 'brothel' patrols, a couple of NCOs and 10 privates in two large lorries with orders to arrest any BOR (British other ranks and NCO) found out of bounds, and plenty were.

This task fell to me one day, patrolling through the village with orders to enter all the brothels and arresting where necessary. Entering a brothel with 3 privates I pushed open a door to find a huge completely naked African at least 6ft 6in tall engaging in that for which he had paid, with an equally naked 4ft 9in Indian girl. On seeing me he promptly deposited the girl on the floor, sprang to attention and saluted me. As he was outside my area of authority, in time honoured army language entirely spontaneously I just said, 'Carry on soldier', whereupon he saluted me again and 'carried on'!!! Word soon got around in the camp and I was regularly greeted 'Morning Sergeant – carry on.'

A notice was posted at the orderly room one day inviting applications for a posting to the Indian Army Ordnance Corp. at a new depot just being set up in far north east India, in Assam. Enquiring further as to when I would be posted – I had then been there 9–10 weeks and was in danger of getting the dreaded 'Deolali Tap' – I was told that a special posting was imminent to join the RTO (Railway Transport Office) in Bombay. This did not appeal to me at all, so much against the wishes of the relevant HQ posting officer (all his work in recommending me for this special job going up the wall) I put my name forward and within 48 hours found myself charged with the task of taking 200 men on a 6 day train journey to Dimapur in Assam. They were a right motley crowd, all medically graded, and including a number of 'Skivers' who I had to put under close arrest every time the train stopped overnight near a town or large village! I was mighty relieved to hand over all my draft on arriving at the base ordnance depot where each man was allocated to one of the various sub units. As I had brought all the individual men's records with me I had to assist in allocating them jobs.

The IAOC officer dealing with this, a Lt. Colonel, then told me that he would like me to join him in the 'provisioning' unit – this being the department which told every other unit what quantities of stores they should hold. Within 10–14 days of starting work, as the job was probably made easier by reason of my previous stock control experience in shops, I was ensconced in his office where we were given sight of top secret papers giving all details of every unit in 14th army, not individually named but in total. Working to a set scale of stock figures we then compared with the previous month's figures and advised each unit of any additions or reductions they should make to their maintenance figures. Very interesting but not very satisfying as one could see no physical results.

The system did sometimes fall down, as it did very spectacularly when we had taken necessary action to bring in spares required to service 160 ten ton American 'MAC' trucks which had just arrived at Bombay. These massively strong trucks with 15 forward and 5 reverse gears were to be used for carrying ammunition and heavy metal tracking used for making airstrips. Unfortunately over 2 months later only 55 arrived at Dimapur, the remainder having been 'written off' by the Indian army transport unit given the task of ferrying them the several thousand miles across India from Bombay!

On one of my sojourns in hospital two drastically different events within days of each other come to mind. I was admitted late one night and put in the only bed available. Feeling very ill, I woke the next morning to see a fellow in the next bed sitting on his bed, feet on the floor, shaving, and I was immediately violently sick. Apparently he had arrived a couple of days earlier, having been one of the last of the Gloucesters evacuated from Rangoon some 10 weeks before. Just after leaving Rangoon he had been shot through both legs, and had spent a nightmare journey back to Dimapur before he had any medical attention and very little food!

He was like a living skeleton, every rib and bone in his body being visible, except for his legs, where both his calves were huge, almost the size of footballs and a mass of sores and ulcers! Yet he was calmly shaving, putting the rest of us to shame! After a couple of days he was on his way back to India, and we never heard further of him. We were later to become quite used to such sights when ex POWs were released, and in fact some 150 were on our ship when we returned to the UK.

The other instance was when one of my colleagues in the RAOC was admitted and put in an adjoining bed. He was quite ill and had to be shaved and given bed baths by the Queen Alexandra nurses. He was deeply engrossed in one of the more lurid type of books always available in hospitals, and did not see the nurse arrive and prepare to wash and shave him. He only emerged from his reading when the sheet was ripped off, the nurse screaming and jumping back, upsetting the bowl of water over the floor. Enough said, except that the nurse asked if she could borrow the book when he had finished with it!!

Meanwhile work proceeded with its perpetual monotony briefly relieved to some degree by twice weekly sessions of housy housy (bingo) held under the light of a lantern, it being pitch dark at about 6.00p.m., until a portable generator was installed, allowing us to have electric light on from dusk until 9.00p.m. nightly.

During one such session a note was delivered to me from the officer commanding with instructions to read it out to the men – about 200 plus strong. Calling a halt to the proceedings I duly read out the note telling us that the war was over in Europe. A short silence then a single voice, 'So what, next number' (rather more colourful language than that however!) Which just about summed up the feelings of all of us – although a few had brothers serving in that theatre of war and were duly grateful.

One job I was given complete control over was the allocation of oxygen (in cylinders) to the various outside engineering units. This created many awkward moments, particularly when I issued a cylinder to a junior NCO, causing the very senior officers in the queue to have kittens!

All had their own special needs – Royal Engineers (bridge building, cutting away blown up bridges etc.) Motor Transport (units repairing motor vehicles, tanks etc.) and so on. The depot produced its own acetylene but this was useless without oxygen which could only be obtained from a huge manufacturing unit in Calcutta. Two major logistical exercises were involved – getting the empty cylinders back from the field units and then transporting them back to Calcutta, subsequently getting the filled cylinders back to Dimapur, the only means of transport being the railway, part narrow gauge track, part broad gauge.

The railway was partly run by the Bengal Railway company and partly by the American Railway units. Everything had to be man-handled on ferries across the River Bramaputra, not possible during the monsoon as huge 150'–300' trees were regularly sweeping downstream, also transferring from narrow gauge railway trucks to broad gauge.

It could take anything from 2 to 4 months for cylinders to reach Calcutta and even longer to get them back as there were always masses of troops and supplies in contention for rail space. When a consignment did arrive, it was only necessary to advise the nearest unit awaiting supplies. Within hours there would be 20–30 quite senior officers on our doorstep all claiming priority! Sometimes 12 cylinders had 40 'priority' customers. I made some good friends – and enemies! Repeated efforts to obtain sufficient extra cylinders being unsuccessful I was given the job of trying to shorten the transportation times. There was no problem at the Calcutta end, where they could turn round cylinders in a matter of hours. An airstrip run by the Americans had been built at Dimapur, one of the first visitors being Earl Mountbatten who addressed a couple of thousand troops when he was made COC 14th Army. Here a single Dakota landed daily bringing mail and other urgent supplies particularly medical. The plane returned to Dum Dum airport Calcutta empty, sometimes taking a seriously ill patient but always being filled with senior officers either going on leave or otherwise being posted back to India.

A system was set up with help of the USAF whereby they would take escorted empty cylinders back to Calcutta so reducing by half the turn round time. Having made the necessary arrangements my officer instructed me (and a pal) to go on the inaugural trip to Calcutta to check that everything was laid on for future missions then proceed on to Bombay for 14 days leave by train, the only leave I ever had in India.

We duly loaded some 25 cylinders onto the plane, the weight of which, added to mine and my corporal pal meant that only 5 of the waiting officers could be taken, leaving some 25 or so on the ground. 2 Corporals, 1 General, 2 L/Colonels and 2 batmen only allowed to board! The USAF crew, two sergeants, had never carried cylinders before and instructed us to lie them down, angling them to stop rolling. The Chin Hills rising to 9,000 feet had to be crossed. There were only fold up bench seats down each side of the plane with the baggage in a separate hold at one end. My very first flight! Almost immediately after taking off the plane banked and the cylinders went rolling first one way then the other – creating loud bangs and 7 very frightened passengers trying to keep our feet out the way.

One of the sergeants came back shouting at us to stop the cylinders rolling or they would smash their way through the side of the plane. We couldn't lash the cylinders in position as the tying points were above waist high, the only alternative was to use the baggage and jam it between cylinders. The officers refused to let us use their baggage so we had to call on the USAF sergeants who, after a few swear words, threw their baggage out to me! I wasn't exactly the most popular NCO in the army that day! It was very necessary though, and within minutes we were hitting air pockets falling hundreds of feet and then shooting up similar distances!

We arrived safely at Dum Dum, where the departing officers

disappeared in a hurry, no thanks! I made necessary transport arrangements for daily consignments much welcomed by BOD staff who used journeys to take their leaves!

After 2 days of cajoling RTO staff we managed to get on a train to Bombay where we arrived after a further 8 days. We had 14 days leave, 4 days to get a train back to Calcutta where we were housed in a transit camp and given instructions to report to the RTO (Railway Transport officer) at Howrah station every morning to see if we could be allocated a space on the next train to Dimapur. At that time Bengal was in the throes of the worst famine ever known, and Indian army trucks were permanently in the streets picking up bodies which were then burnt.

Walking to Howrah station one day, my pal tripped over a sack lying on the pavement, kicking it into the gutter to find that it was in fact the corpse of a baby which had obviously been lying there for days.

I decided there and then – no more leave in India for me. I did have one memorable experience on leave, a notice was put up in our leave hotel inviting footballers to take part in a match against a newly arrived RAF team at Bombay stadium. I turned out and had a good match although being frequently frustrated by a huge goalkeeper in the RAF team who admitted, after being confronted in the changing room after the match, to being one Ted Ditchburn of Tottenham Hotspur whose last game prior to embarking had been for England!!

We learnt that just previous to arriving in Bombay on leave, there had been what was probably the biggest disaster of the entire war. A large cargo ship carrying ammunition had just arrived from America, had caught fire and exploded resulting in all the ships in dock being totally destroyed and rendering it out of action for many months. Certainly a large area of

Bombay was out of bounds to us all. (Hand of fate again as the RTO unit I was destined to be posted to was completely wiped out!)

Not long after getting back to the depot from my Bombay leave, I received a letter from home telling me my sister Nore had died in mid January 1945. I immediately wrote back saying that I hoped it had not upset my father too much, to my dismay receiving a further letter dated a week previous to that above saying my father had died, this being four days before Nore's death.

Within weeks I received another letter telling me that my eldest sister Addy, who had two sons and a daughter, had lost her eldest son Peter who was killed instantly and sister and brother badly injured. They had been playing in a 'den' they had built in a field behind their house with a mortar shell given them in all innocence by an American soldier who said it was a 'dud' practice round. When the children, aged 10, 11 and 14 didn't come home, neighbours reported hearing a bang and a search revealed what had happened.

The American army paid my sister a very modest sum in respect of the injuries to the survivors but totally refused to compensate for Peter's death, saying that as he was not of working age and therefore not contributing to the family income, compensation was NOT relevant!

We had been receiving a few reinforcements direct from UK and it fell to me to interview them and post them to suitable jobs in the depot. As frequently happened newcomers brought UK newspapers with them these being very much in demand. One was a Cornish paper and I was distressed to read that my old pal Dennis Mathews (Math) had been killed and there was an account of his military funeral. I was to learn later that my old unit had been stationed at St. Margaret's Bay and a truck load of men were getting off the lorry outside the cinema in Dover when they received a direct hit from a cross channel shell, killing Dennis, his great pal and mine, Frankie Gardner (whose grave in Greenbank Cemetery, Bristol, I visited after the war) and several other of my old pals as well as 4 or 5 men who had joined after I had left and I didn't know – also injuring many more. Another instance of the vagaries of fate!

We worked long hours at the base ordnance depot, 6½ days a week, half day Sundays. Housed in canvas 'bashas' our wooden beds were about 3ft off the hardened mud floor, with racks to hold our kit about 60" high. We soon found out why with the onset of the monsoon, water some 12"–18" deep rushing through our bashas for days on end. Woe betied anyone who left clothing or kit on the floor.

We had our own cookhouse and mess tent with native cooks who were very good. We had to collect rations twice a week for all 200 of us from a supplies unit some 5 miles away, usually all tinned items but occasionally fresh meat, live chicken, sheep or goats, all of which had to be in the cooking pot within two hours of being killed!

Bread was also collected, this having been baked in an open field bakehouse where it was impossible to prevent flies, mostly bluebottles, from being cooked into the loaves, making them look like currant loaves. The main meal was just after dark at about 6.30p.m., but by popular request this was brought forward by an hour so that the meal could be eaten in daylight. This lasted 3 days, then we reverted to 6.30p.m. the reason being the chaps were spending so much time and wasting so much bread picking out the flies, that it was agreed that cooked flies were preferable to starving men!

Very much against orders we used winches on MT recovery lorries to pull down enough trees to make a small football pitch about 75yds × 40yds. This was in use almost all day by adjacent units for 7-a-side games. We reserved 5.30 to 6.15 every day for our own use and matches were arranged every evening. I had previously written to Stanley Rous, FA Secretary (who actually refereed the very last football match we played before leaving England long before he rose to his elevated position) asking him to send us some rules of football handbooks. He sent 6 of which I kept one and distributed the remainder. From that time on I either played or refereed a match every day, including full time matches on a full size pitch near the airfield on most Sunday afternoons when we played other depots.

No football boots were allowed (or available), we wore daps (sandals) with lashings made from webbing removed from our beds, no jerseys, one team wore shirts, the other no shirts. We played right through the monsoon, frequently just kick abouts played in the mud, nude, as this was very good treatment for the all too prevalent prickly heat. No need for modesty – no women within miles! One Sunday afternoon there was no football match so 4 or 5 of us armed ourselves with rifles and went into the surrounding jungle where we had heard reports that wild chicken had been seen. Sure enough we found them roosting in branches some 10 feet off the ground. The trouble was you had to shoot them on their way down, once they reached the ground they shot off at speed and it was impossible to shoot them. After firing about 80–100 rounds we finally got one. Back in camp, we gave it to our cook who expressed surprise that we had caught one, especially as it weighed 7 or 8lbs. He made us a superb curry, no doubt using innards and all which he confirmed later after we had dined!

One of my pals couldn't drive and as I had managed to obtain a third line (not fit for use!) ambulance for transporting our football team I took him on runs up the Manipar Road towards Kohima, a single track unpaved road with drop of up to 1,000 feet on one side, similar upwards on the other! A little bit scary even for a skilled driver – particularly as the large majority of military Indian drivers were anything but experienced! There were passing places every mile or so when it was obligatory for vehicles going in certain directions at specified times to halt. It was also obligatory for all vehicles to pick up anyone hitching a ride as they were inevitably service personnel.

On one such drive, teaching my pal to drive, we pulled into a passing place behind a convoy of trucks. When we moved off we had only just turned into the main road when we all had to stop. We didn't move for some time, so I went forward to find the truck third in front of ours had crashed into the preceeding truck and there were about 12 men congregated around the driver's door, all jabbering away. Pushing through and asking why the delay eventually I was taken to the back of the truck where I could see an Indian crushed between the two trucks. The argument was about who was to blame. I jumped up into the rear truck and reversed back expecting the body to drop to the ground. It didn't, so we pulled it off, the towing hook having gone right through his body. Apparently he had run out and tried to climb over the tailboard, being crushed when the driver of the front vehicle missed his gear and stopped.

I made them put the body in the back of the truck and eventually we got under way again. Life is cheap in India – even cheaper during war!

We were paid a visit by Denis Compton's touring football team composed entirely of internationals including Ted Ditchburn in goal. I managed to make the L of C (Line of Communication) team, playing at right back directly opposite

Denis Compton who repeatedly made a mug of me! We only had one good player, an Indian who had represented his country, all the rest were amateurs, hence 9:0 loss!

Before and during the interval, Freddie Mills and Jack London gave a boxing exhibition. To round off the week Vera Lynn gave a 2 hour concert standing in the back of a 3 ton truck and was rapturously received. The only other celebrity ever to visit us was Evelyn Laye. But we did have pictures once a month – never mind that they were Indian – to help us keep our sanity!!

The USAF airfield, although with a permanent staff of 5 or 6, had every facility, cinema, small swimming pool, refrigerator – but best of all as far as we were concerned, they invited us to collect fresh cold water every day. We used to send a truck loaded with 'Chagris', goat skin water bottles, which kept water really cold as long as it was kept hanging up in the sun!

During another spell in a tented hospital with pneumonia and malaria, one night I experienced my first earthquake, about 20 of us waking up to find ourselves decanted onto the floor minus our mosquito nets. When I returned to the depot my officer arranged for me to relieve an RAOC NCO at Kohima whilst he went on leave, this as a sort of rehabilitation leave. I spent four weeks then returned to Dimapur. Six days later the Japs overran Kohima sparking off one of the worst battles during the entire Burma Campaign. Again fate was very much on my side, my old regiment was in the forefront in the subsequent battle to regain the bare hilltops comprising what was then a small village of some 1,500 people. There are 192 men who went to India with me buried in the huge beautifully kept War Cemetery, now on the site of the notorious D.C. (District Commissioners) tennis court. The Japs reached a point less than 20 miles from Dimapur. Had

The author in 1994 on the former site of IAOD Depot, Kohima.

they not been stopped there, they would have overrun India as there was a huge complex of supplies depots virtually undefended at Dimapur – everything from food to amm-unition, petrol and our BOD with some 3,000 workers which held every conceivable item as well as the air strip a few miles away.

My officer asked me if I would like to be put forward for a commission then did so. The position was that as a War Substantive Corporal, I could not be reduced to the ranks and

*Kohima Cemetery
where 192 Dorset
men are buried.*

so, although not in my unit, I was still on their strength, meaning that they were one corporal short in their ranks. Equally I couldn't be promoted as they would then be a sergeant short. Eventually, shortly after we were moved to Rangoon, I was offered a direct commission as Captain – in the Indian Army – requiring me to sign on for two years – or the duration of the war – whichever was the longer. As by then I had been nearly 4 years abroad, it didn't take me long to decline!

When the fourteenth army was approaching Rangoon via Kohima and Imphal I was detailed with a party of 20 other ranks to take a train load of vital stores to Calcutta and arrange their transport to Rangoon. Our main function was to oversee the transfer of goods across the river Bramaputra, between trains and, most important of all, to prevent the trains from being boarded by Indians who would climb on board and throw anything they could off the train without caring what it was. Every time the train was due to stop the driver gave a triple burst on his whistle warning us so that as soon as the train halted escorts filed out of the goods wagon we were travelling in and with loaded rifles, sometimes fired and repelled invaders! As before mentioned, the Americans ran the railway for the most part. When we reached the river, we put on a couple of wagon loads of equipment and I detailed two men to take all their equipment, load goods on the other side of the river and wait for the remainder of us. Sublime optimism, when we reached the other side no sign of the trucks or my two men. I found out that the Yanks had hitched our trucks to a waiting train completing its complement and then promptly despatched it, including our two chaps – Destination: Delhi!!! They eventually turned up at Calcutta without their trucks nearly three weeks later!!

During one of our frequent halts pulled into railway siding passing places we received a single whistle blast warning us that we would shortly be on the move, only to stop again almost immediately, chaps posted outside again, and no sign of movement. I went forward to find the driver and his mate (both Anglo Indians) digging a hole in the railway embankment. When I asked why the gardening they drew my attention to the body of an Indian a couple of trucks back. He had run out to try and climb aboard, fell and was cut in half, 2 legs and 1 arm, 1 arm and the head. I sent a couple of chaps to help with the digging of the grave. Right at the back of the train was a passenger coach carrying 10 USA airmen. They found out what had happened then they put the two parts on the bank and took turns at photographing groups crouched behind it! Really put me off Yanks forever! Four of our officers had asked me to try and 'smuggle' their jeeps into Rangoon and I said I would do so if possible, hence I agreed to transport them to the depot being established in Rangoon.

We were at Calcutta for several weeks, visiting the docks every day and arranging to send 'bit' loads and escort where possible. We quickly ran out of cash, not being able to draw wages and were broke when one of the chaps said he would see if he could sell the Jeeps to some Yanks he had met in a night club. This he managed to do, providing enough cash for us to really enjoy the rest of the time until we left with the remaining six of the escort and stores on a ship to Rangoon. All went well until early one morning I was shaken awake by one of the escort who told me his mate had gone berserk, raced up onto deck and jumped overboard.

The ship's captain said there was no point in searching in the pitch dark as anything dropped over the side in the Rangoon river was immediately sucked down by the undercurrent, as he proved by throwing an empty box over the side.

Approaching the dock, this 48 hours after we had taken Rangoon, there were a few shots fired, I don't know who at but one of the ships crew manning the Bofors guns said he had seen a flash from one of the Stothart & Pitt cranes on the docks. Whereupon all 6 of the BOFORS (Ack Ack guns) opened up completely wrecking all the cranes. No more problems except that when we were later given the task of unloading the ship we had to rely entirely on the ship's derricks plus one old Coles jib crane.

Ashore we were housed for a few weeks in the very posh Burmese Stock Exchange building whilst the new depot was being established a few miles out of town at Monkey Point, deemed a good site as situated on the junction of the Rangoon river and a tributary, with land border of only about ½ mile and water on all other sides, so deterring anticipated attempts at pilferage.

As senior NCO it fell to me on landing to carry out the normal army procedures of auctioning the possessions of the unfortunate chap lost on the voyage and I always marvelled at how well all ranks supported the auction. As usual, there were very few belongings, shoe polish and brushes, unused toothpaste, soap etc. plus a few items of clothing, bush hat, belts, socks, with the biggest item a small tin trunk which we all had as our belongings were reasonably safe from red ants if held in one.

This tin raised over 250 rupees (about 15 rupees to £), the shoe polish 50 rupees (cost from our army shop was 2 rupees), with almost all those outbid, throwing the money bid unsuccessfully into a kitbag collecting all monies. Nearly £800 was finally raised and as we were restricted to £40 in what we could send home every 3 months, I had to get special permission from the relevant authorities before I could send the money to his mother in Sheffield.

I was given the task of transferring goods from the ship to this new depot. The quay was reinforced concrete built out over the river with huge holes all over the place where we had bombed it during preceding years. We lost several local labourers who tripped over the tangled steel re-inforcing rods around the bomb craters, they fell into the river and simply disappeared. We did manage to arrange crates and bales around the most vulnerable holes and this avoided further falls. Using the ship's derricks we managed to unload everything, mostly directly onto lorries but also 12 fork lift trucks, which we towed to an adjacent road knowing they couldn't be pinched, ensuring that the smaller cases were sent to the depot first. None of us had ever seen a fork lift truck before. The time came to load them so I arranged for our sole Coles crane to pick one up, the lorry to move beneath to load it.

I duly fitted slings to the fork lift and crane and told the driver to lift. Nothing happened so I looked round to berate the Burmese crane driver, and saw that the crane's front wheels were 2 feet in the air. Hastily dropping his load I checked the weight of the fork lift – 9½ tons – Coles crane maximum lift 3 tons! No future there, so it fell to me to tow them the four miles to the depot with me driving the fork lift truck which had rear wheel steering. None of the locals would drive, particularly as the roads were all badly cratered with broken water mains flooding huge areas making it difficult to see the craters! It took us 3 days to complete this job alone! One day we were told to arrange an escort to the local airfield, duly escorting a small convoy of staff cars.

We were then dismissed but not before we found out that the staff cars were to meet the Japanese delegation arriving to sign the end of war declaration, the first time we had any inkling that the end of our war was imminent! At about 2.00a.m. the next morning, we were awoken by shooting and ships' sirens to learn that the war was over. We had nothing to celebrate with so about 40 of us filed into jeeps and visited the half dozen officers messes housing our IAOC officers. The first one invited us in and we quickly emptied their drinks cupboard. We left to go to the next larger mess, realising when we arrived that they had been warned we were on our way, the gates were closed and locked with a single sentry outside who had been ordered to refuse us entry. One against 40 – no chance, the gates were taken off hinges, doors were forced and again all drink consumed.

Then to the next mess – similar reception – similar result – except that I don't remember what happened afterwards. Apparently the 6th mess was lucky, no one survived that long!

Days later we were moved into an empty house much closer to the new depot opposite what had been a pre-war petrol depot handling exports from Burma oil wells loading onto tankers. No such activity now, everything had been blown up, but enough overhead pipework and concrete areas remained to encourage the development of the site as a depot to handle petrol coming *into* Burma by tanker, unloading into newly positioned shore tanks with hundreds of Burmese and Indian soldiers filling thousands of 4 gallon jerry cans for distribution by road. We used to go back to the billet for our midday meal and on our way to lunch one day when we were about a mile away, there was a huge explosion, followed by dozens of others, with a huge ball of smoke above the site.

We immediately realised what had happened, in fact were almost expecting it. Jerry cans were filled by hand from ordinary brass taps as used for water, fuelled from the overhead pipes. There were some 300–400 such taps. Petrol was spilled all over the place and it was inevitable that a spark or someone smoking would set it ablaze. We never knew which, the unfortunates working there had no chance of surviving. Very few could escape on the land side, on the other side was the Rangoon river, a choice between being burnt to death or jumping into the river to put out their burning clothes knowing that they then would risk almost certain death by drowning. The reason for the explosion and number of casualties was never made public, probably too many heads would have rolled but certainly the depot was never re-opened.

There was almost a riot amongst my fellow other ranks, still over 150 left from those who went to Dimapur with me, when we were addressed by the officer commanding the IAOC depot who said that as we would all be going home sometime during the next six months, he had arranged for an equal number of replacements to join us direct from England. As they had only been in the army a few weeks he was relying on us to teach them their jobs.

There were only 6 or 7 NCOs in our ranks, 3 corporals and 3 or 4 lance corporals – and all were on basic pay for their rank. There was no disagreement at this stage but when the newcomers arrived a few days later they were all promoted to sergeants with sergeants' pay because they were on the strength of the units they had left in the UK. And this with the longest serving Sergeant with 5 weeks service! We realised it wasn't their fault and work went on almost as usual, leaving the newcomers to learn by example.

This quickly changed when a couple of chaps were put on charge by two of these new sergeants – one for kicking a (holy) cow trying to eat his dinner from his plate when going from cookhouse to dining hall (a very common occurrence), the other for using bad language when remonstrated with! Sick parades escalated suddenly and co-operation became NIL when both charges were upheld and jankers given. I had never had to deal with jankers in the IOAC before so needless to say I wasn't going to start now, although I had to make my point, and those of all my chaps known to the OC in due course. Which made the men all the more determined than ever, very few of the new sergeants learnt much by watching our chaps from that day on!

We had another visit by Denis Compton's football team although I didn't get a game as we had not had time for football in Rangoon. I did get out to see the match, including Freddie Mills and Jack London, the latter two agreeing to join us at our local canteen which was beneath the 'Swadagong Pagoda'. A bit of a farce to call it a canteen as there were no NAAFIs in the far east, just unit canteens run by senior warrant officers! We could buy cups of tea (char), jam, corned beef and Maconachies (stew) sandwiches, all army rations except for the bread! We had a great time, particularly with Freddie Mills who was a genuinely nice chap, his party piece being a rendering of Merzy Doates and Maisey Doates dressed as a 6 year old girl!

In late October, we were all told we should be going home within a few weeks. When we learnt that Rangoon racecourse was being re-opened we all drew some pay (we hadn't drawn any for months as nothing to buy, we could only use it for housey housey and gambling) and decided to go racing. There were only half a dozen horses in one race – all the other races were for laughs: a naval rating pulling a rickshaw carrying another rating, RAF ditto, Army etc. – all duly weighed in and with outrageous bets placed on them on a Tote run by army officers! Rickshaws were pulled by real Burmese with passengers being weighed, bullock carts and so on.

None of us came away winners, this being restricted to the officers running the Tote! We spent a last visit to the local bazaar buying junk as the money we were using was only legal tender in Burma, only to find out when we embarked on the *Empress of India* a few days later that we could change it into English money, albeit at a very discounted price!

There were a couple of hundred ex-Japanese prisoners of war on the boat and what a state they were in. It made us realise how lucky we were. We were asked to do what we could to make their life more comfortable but most were hospitalised and outside our reach. A short stop at Colombo then home through the Suez canal where I bought a real leather wallet for 6d and I am still using it today, 54 years later! Going through the Med. we were treated to the spectacle of a water spout, when we all, about 2,000 men, rushed to one side causing tannoy instruction to even ourselves out as we were causing problems when the ship veered away to miss it.

The ship arrived at Liverpool on a bitterly cold day. We had been issued with UK kit so all had greatcoats and were wrapped in blankets when on deck approaching the docks. Everyone was feeling very emotional, this being broken when one chap pronounced, 'If those bloody dockers are in shirt sleeves, I'm staying on board and going back to India.' Fortunately they too were really wrapped up. On disembarking we were all given rail vouchers back to our UK depots.

I was the only Dorset on board and travelled to Dorchester via London, arriving at Dorchester three hours after the main body of my unit the 2nd Dorsets had returned, they having been given a rousing reception when marching behind a band through the streets to the top of town depot.

I felt quite weary and lonely, trudging the same journey on my own, carrying all my kit. Then I met, after many years, many of my old mates learning at first hand of the happenings at Kohima and my old 5th Battalion in Europe.

I was given repatriation leave until after Christmas, when I reported back to Dorchester. As a consequence of my IAOC experience I was posted as a pay sergeant to the Combined operations Experimental Establishment at Westward Ho, North Devon. I had no experience of this job, but was shown the ropes by Freda, an ATS clerk, and soon learnt the job. Apart from several hundred soldiers, there were equal number of civilian employees and it was my very first involvement with the ramifications of PAYE.

Feeling my feet, and with a certain amount of arrogance as none of the officers in charge had served abroad, or in fact for any length of time, I found that pay parade was always held at 5.00p.m. on Fridays after men had worked a full day. I had already ascertained that there was a train to Bristol leaving Barnstaple at 1.00p.m. every Friday so I immediately told my pay officer that I was changing pay parade to 11.00a.m. so that the men could return to work after the midday meal! I also arranged for a DR (motor cycle) to be available to run me into Barnstaple at 12.15p.m. All worked OK for the first time but during the following week my clerk told me her boyfriend, Bill Shorthouse, (later to play centre half for England) wanted to go home to Wolverhampton every weekend to play for Wolverhampton reserves, so I scrapped the DR for a truck, and 3 more passengers! Bill had a hectic weekend every week, travel to Wolverhampton, then frequently on to places like Preston, Leeds, Sunderland etc., return to Wolverhampton late Saturday night, leave again Sunday morning meeting me at Bristol Temple Meads and on to Bideford via Exeter. He always got rail tickets from the Wolves. I had no such luck, so had to work a real fiddle to avoid paying for the train journey to Bristol and back every week. Part of this involved running up (or down) platforms at stopping stations en-route to bye pass the ticket inspector. Arriving at Bideford at about

5.30a.m., about 50 returning troops rushed the ticket barrier where the inspector accepted anything you cared to put in his hand, rail ticket (the exception), tram/bus ticket, 6d, 1/– (if flush!) and then to pile in to a 3 ton truck for journey back to quarters, having previously arranged for this vehicle to be waiting, just meeting the 6.00a.m. pass expiry time. I had no problem in getting passes, I made them out myself and could always persuade some officer to sign them – plus rail passes every 5 or 6 weeks!

Bill Shorthouse duly married Freda when he left the army. Some 35 years later when answering a query from a hospital official, I learnt that he was Bill's son and that Freda had only recently died!

Whilst still in Burma I had written to my pre-war employers, the Britannic Assurance company, thanking them for paying me a small salary (I think it was 8/– a week) throughout my time in the army, but telling them I had no intention of returning to them after the war. I received a very nice reply, accepting my decision and saying they would continue the payments until my discharge, which they did. So when at home during weekends, I started job hunting, admitting that I turned down one offer from a large wholesaler in the grocery trade, I wanted a completely fresh challenge.

In May 1946 I was demobbed, 6½ years after being conscripted, probably having established a record of sorts for a conscripted soldier, over 6 years as a corporal. During this time I never once put anyone on a charge, always preferring to reprimand and talk to any transgressor, suggesting they mend their ways rather than put them before the officer in charge who would offer similar advice plus a punishment! On reflection, probably the military way of enforcing discipline was the correct one, fortunately it never fell to me to check this out! I picked up the dreaded pin strip suit plus shirt, 2 vests and underpants plus socks and a pair of shoes, declining the free issue Trilby hat, the only hat I ever liked was the bush hat – Australian type! I then moved into my father-in-law's house at Horfield, Bristol.

I also bought my first house, taking over an existing mortgage of about £500 on a house costing £675 using my war gratuity of about £260 less £85 deducted to cover the cost of having Glad's widows' pension stamps brought up to date – these having been put on hold whilst I was a serving soldier!

Another amusing event, in retrospect, was my first attempt at DIY in my first house in Bristol. We only had cold water and an old china sink. I obtained (no questions asked) a gas geyser to provide hot water over the sink. One Sunday morning I turned off the water stop tap beneath the well mat inside the front door and stripped down the existing piping, replastering the wall as necessary and putting the geyser in position. About midday there was a knock at the front door – half a dozen neighbours wanted to know if I had turned the water off – apparently this also meant 6 adjoining houses also had no water. I had to tell them it would take another 2–3 hours, could only apologise and ask them to get water from a neighbour on the opposite side of the road!

I caused further slight controversy later when I decided to re-point the stone walling front, having to chip out the old mortar which created clouds of dust. I had to knock at neighbours' doors to warn them each time I started work so that they could close their windows!

When completed the re-pointing improved the appearance of the house considerably, unfortunately to the detriment of adjoining houses!

Although not related to the above, we had the opportunity

of buying a house at Hanham Green at a good price as it belonged to a relative of a workmate and I bought it before it was actually put on the market, only to move a year later to the Ashton district to be closer to my work and not requiring a 10 mile bike or bus ride each way every day.

Prior to leaving the army I took a driving test so as to obtain a civilian driving licence thinking my future might lie in that direction. I had to take my test in a 20 ton breakdown lorry complete with crane, driving around the hilly narrow streets of Bideford! Thankfully I passed, no doubt due to the many different vehicles I had driven in India, from jeeps to tanks and everything in between!

Eventually, thanks to my brother-in-law Arthur, I obtained a job with the Ministry of Works (now Dept of Environment) plant maintenance depot in Bristol, shortly afterwards moving to my house at Fishponds, Bristol.

In a corner of the MOW site, completely hidden by undergrowth and blackberry bushes we found about 20 forty gallon metal drums, all filled with something. Curiosity led us to retrieve them, and we found a varied mix of contents, various oils, paint, creosote and white spirit. Obviously it was not acceptable to leave such flammable materials within the depot, so the staff took it upon themselves to clear the site! One of the drums contained a very high gloss brown paint, very acceptable, although Glad wasn't altogether appreciative of having a house painted brown inside and out! Neither was I when I found the first time it rained that it was a water based paint, meant for indoor use only! Still it did act quite well as a base coat, if promptly sealed and repainted!

When I was working at MOW Bristol Depot we had one employee, a crane driver, who was given the title of 'The Honest Rogue'. If anyone wanted anything, particularly in the building sphere, wood, bricks, tiles, cement just ask 'Wilkie' and it would appear within days. This was at a time when everything was in very short supply after the war, and always at acceptable (favourable) prices! But no questions asked please!

I met up with him several years after the MOW depot closed. He was then working for the Co-op as a milkman and proudly showed me his float, neatly divided in two sections, one carrying milk, the other Wilkie's section: anything from groceries, cigarettes, greengrocery, all available at ordinary shop prices. I always wondered if the success of this private enterprise eventually led to the Co-op and other milk purveyors adding these items to all their floats as is now commonplace!

Shortly before moving into the house, following my discharge in mid summer 1946, having served just over 6½ years, I was blessed with my first son, Brian. Glad had a very trying and potentially dangerous pregnancy, for the last 6 months having to attend Southmead Hospital daily to have treatment, something involving wheat germ oil, but everything turned out OK.

I had 6 attacks of malaria when in India and Burma, being hospitalised once, the other times being spent in battalion/unit sick bays, but when back in England and on disembarkation leave, I had further bad attack. Glad called in her own doctor who treated me with what he said was a new injection instead of the normal mepacrine.

It certainly worked then and since, as I have never again had malaria!

Throwing myself whole heartedly into my job which I found most interesting, and where my IAOC work came in useful, once again I found myself quickly put in charge of requisitioning spares necessary to keep heavy plant in working order. At that time, pre-fab houses were being built at a great speed. The depot provided cranes, excavators, bulldozers, concrete mixers, dump trucks necessary to prepare sites over an area stretching from Southampton up to Oxford and across to West Wales and South West of England, all served from factories making the actual pre-fabs at Gloucester and Weston-Super-Mare. Sourcing spares was a real problem, first to identify the parts required (American, Canadian or British machines) then sourcing supplies from USA army depots, UK army depots, British manufacturers (the easy ones!) then getting them – all providing a real challenge. A couple of months after starting work the government initiated a drive to enlist permanent civil servants. I applied and after an all day entrance exam at the Co-op hall in Bristol, was successful and was duly appointed class 1 clerk civil servant, retaining my existing job at a slightly increased salary. I was also told that my war service would count double when the time came for me to retire – a 13 year start, I thought – although this was never confirmed. My work involved frequent visits to sites to discuss with site engineers what plant was best suited to their needs, plus those to identify and collect spares from depots, works from Manchester to the Home Counties. I really thought I had found my niche in life, a regular safe job with a good pension at the end. The very bad weather in spring of 1947 led me to eventually think otherwise.

The UK had frozen for months on end and work on sites was severely restricted, none more so than at several large sites at Plymouth where work carried on but the huge frozen rutted sites played havoc with the plant particularly with dumpers, causing broken steering handwheels, columns and linkages where drivers tried to force their way around sites.

After heavy pressure from the sites warning that work would

soon grind to a halt unless spares were forthcoming for the dumpers I found that the engineering works making these parts, near Altrincham in Cheshire, had our orders and had our spares, but they had no way of selecting them and getting them to us, and so they jumped at the suggestion when I said we could collect, saying they would give us carte blanche if we could identify and load the stores onto our vehicle.

Consequently a driver and myself set off in a 5 ton open lorry at 3.00a.m. one morning, arriving after a terrible journey some 10 hours later, changing drivers every hour or so. An hour and half sorting and loading spares then we set out on return journey, which was much easier as the heavy load made the driving easier. Reaching Bristol at midnight, I dropped off the driver at his home, taking the lorry home and back to the depot at 6.30a.m. next morning, handing the lorry over to the first driver to report to work, him taking the lorry to Plymouth.

There followed glowing reports back from the site at Plymouth, culminating in a visit from the regional director who told me to put in for overtime. This I did and received a letter back from a regional finance officer (which I have always regretted not keeping) saying that according to my report I had spent about 21 hours on the trip, plus 3 hours next morning, of which about 22 hours had been spent driving and as a passenger. I was employed as a Grade 1 clerk therefore had spent only 2 hours doing my job. The letter instructed me to put in an application for half a day's leave – this being quite generous treatment! I showed this letter to the regional director who went berserk, sending a copy to the Minister of Works in London. I eventually received my overtime but this really alerted me to the Civil Service way of life where there is a hard and fast set of rules governing every circumstance never to be ignored.

In late 1947/48 the government made the decision to disband the plant division and return it to the civilian domain. After dispersing the plant all over the UK to civil and private buyers (with some misgivings as to the propriety of some deals!) I was posted to the MOW offices in Bristol and put in charge of supplies to all the ancient monuments in the same area as before. Instead of handling cranes, excavators etc., I found myself dealing with requests to supply 1 spade, 2 brooms and a wheelbarrow to Stonehenge for example, work which took me at most half an hour a day, spending the rest of my time helping a colleague to produce useless sets of statistics required weekly by head office in London! This ceased when we received a visit from an organisation and methods team from London who found that the reams of statistical reports were never looked at in London and were merely filed. My colleague transferred to another department, I handed in my resignation, joining 2 former workmates at the depot who had started a small garage business.

Soon I found that this was another mistake on my part, as I found myself working 80/90 hours a week – my colleagues about a tenth of these hours! I was living on my savings as the business was not exactly a gold mine!

I was sorely tempted when I received a letter from my friend, the MOW finance officer, inviting me to return, when I would be instantly transferred to the newly established dept of Insurance and Pensions where my pre-war work experience would prove useful. He gave me 14 days to accept when I would be deemed not to have left and thus have uninterrupted service.

My experience of the Civil Service mentality decided me NOT to return – much to the annoyance of Glad's brother,

Arthur, who thought I should as I would have been in at the start of a huge new department. He was probably right at the time but I could not face up to the frustrations which I knew would arise as a member of the Civil Service.

In later years I learnt that the clerk who was transferred prior to my leaving the Civil Service eventually rose to be head of the west of England division – and he was an idiot! But he had a good memory of where to look for regulations governing his area of work!

One of our customers at the garage, who owned a thriving office equipment business, asked us to start making filing equipment and this turned round our fortunes. However, not through any efforts of my partners who worked less and less. Shortly afterwards, I was offered a job with this office equipment firm at the then unheard of wage of £10 a week, as against the £3.16.0 a week I received as a civil servant! I jumped at it and soon found myself once again finding my IAOC experience invaluable. It was part of my job to place orders with 5 or 6 small engineering works spread as far afield as London, Swindon, Cardiff and Bristol for a wide range of filing cabinets all made on different types of plant (some very Heath Robinson) and, more important, in widely varying paint finishing processes, varying from air drying to infra red and convection ovens. The result was that there was a huge variation in the colour of the finished products, making it extremely difficult to match-up when required to make big assemblies. I had to wipe three of the manufacturers off the list as they were never going to make compatible items which could safely be blended with products from the other sources. My office equipment company decided to exhibit in the first exhibition to take place after the war at Olympia and it fell to me to take a huge load of office equipment and set up our stand. The first problem was to find space to park near Olympia – this was solved when a departing driver told me to seek out a certain police officer which I did and found a space right next to the nearest door to our stand – but £10 the poorer! Did I help start police corruption?

It was a very successful exhibition with almost a monopoly of the type of equipment offered, mostly aimed at doctors, dentists and school medical record departments who had to find some means of storing the medical records just introduced as a result of the new National Health Service. Now everyone in the country had to be registered with doctors and dentists and so had medical record cards accordingly.

The business soon attracted numerous hangers-on, all of whom seemed to work busily when the boss was around but had the ability to be able to switch to nothingness as soon as he was out of sight. But they were very good company during the very long parties spent entertaining supposed business guests every night – and early mornings when at exhibitions!

When working for the office equipment firm, the owner once told me over a meal when he had drunk rather well, that I was blessed with an agile mind and an abundance of common sense, even if no education. It was up to me to use both to the best advantage, when I would not need to work for him, rather the reverse and he would not be adverse to working for me!

Another time he said I was very stubborn and not easily swayed once my mind was made up. Others have also said the same thing, so there must be some truth in it. Certainly I do not find it easy to suffer fools lightly, and am not adverse to telling them so, although for reasons of diplomacy I have frequently had to bite my tongue and stifle my real feelings.

Reverting to the most necessary job of meeting promised delivery dates, this also had its strange moments – like when a doctor in Bristol said he had received three very large consignments of the cabinets etc. he had ordered, all during the space of 10 days prior to my taking on this job. It appeared that the system which had been used was rather faulty to say the least! All goods were delivered direct from the factories to a timber merchant in Bristol. When orders were received from doctors the only paperwork which was raised was a label for every item required for that doctor. These were sent to the timber yard men who packed and despatched the goods. Where it fell down, was that the packer made 2 or 3 different size of packing crate, packing say 12 items in each crate but using only 2 labels. Surplus labels were returned to the office who assumed they had been sent back in error and returned them to the packers, who in turn assumed it was a new order and promptly packed and sent off another batch, again returning surplus labels to the office, who equally promptly sent them back again and so on! Just how many duplicated and triplicated orders were not reported back to us is anyone's guess, several dozen consignments so returned were probably only the tip of the iceberg!!

A rather strange case which rather tickled my fancy occurred when a representative took a large order from a dental practice which wanted everything painted to match the existing equipment and so borrowed a drawer showing the colour to be matched. The paint shop was duly instructed and goods and drawer delivered to the surgery.

Calling at the paint shop a day or so later I enquired how the matching had gone to be told they hadn't been able to get anything near the correct shade so they had repainted the drawer and so achieved a perfect match! It must have worked or the dentist was so pleased to eventually get his order that no complaint was ever received! Amidst all this inefficiency and chaos it was inevitable that trouble loomed, which it did and the boss arranged a moratorium whereby all debts were held in abeyance for 12 months, all fresh deliveries having to be paid for on the dot. Basic problems still existed, however – too many non-earners drawing good salaries with cars and generous expenses. Within 3 or 4 months the receivers were called in and I found myself having to co-operate with them. They quickly found a buyer, a London accountant to take over the business. I did not exactly take to this man, especially when I was told to attend a board meeting in London. This actually took place in the Treasury where I found out he was a high ranking official and must have been to be able to hold meetings there! Within 4 or 5 months we were in trouble again, I couldn't get supplies and personal visits to all suppliers revealed that they had not received any payments since the company had been taken over and they had all been fooled when this new boss had personally visited them and spun a tale, asking them to support him for 3 or 4 months whilst I re-organised and they would get both past monies and that for new supplies. Instead they got nothing and within weeks we were back to square one and bankrupt again. Which made me wonder what collusion there had been between the treasury official and the receiver!

I was being paid by the new receiver to carry on and meet existing and new orders where possible to keep money coming in, but decided enough was enough and resigned, having been asked by my two previous associates to rejoin them in a company they had set up manufacturing sheet metal products for several Bristol companies, I did, but insisted that this company be made into a limited company, which was done.

I was confident that I could profit from my past experiences and sold my house. I had moved several times since leaving the army – invariably making a profit on each house. I bought a smaller less expensive property which enabled me to put £800 into the new venture. Once again this proved to be a mistake, my new co-directors appointed two further directors, both non active and non experienced, thus 5 directors and 3 employees – with the 'working' directors, one about 10 hours a week, another 15/20 hours and muggins about 85/90 hours. I was appointed Sales Director at one of the weekly board meetings. It made no difference to me, I went out and got the orders, came back and worked like hell to meet deadlines and produce the jobs, nearly always having to deliver them and wait until I collected cash or cheque, returning via the bank to cash the cheques and then pay our staff. I did this for some six months during which time I had drummed up quite a few orders from local hospitals which encouraged me to investigate further what opportunities there could be in that field. One of the jobs we took on was reconditioning hospital equipment, usually in very bad decorative order but which could be brought back to very good condition at quite a low cost. We eventually moved to treating beds, first removing the paint by dipping them in a large tank of caustic soda, after which we had to hose them down to remove all traces of caustic. This was not a very satisfactory process which we solved by throwing the beds overnight in a nearby stream, getting them out in the morning before anyone was around! It proved to be a very slow operation and as prospects in this direction looked promising we used a local firm – still going strong – to shot blast them.

After numerous journeys delivering and collecting beds from the shot blasters and keeping eyes and ears open to see what plant was required, we enlisted part time help from a chap with real experience and built our own shot blasting plant. This made a tremendous difference to our turn around and throughput, the only snag being that as the home made plant would not have passed insurance and explosion tests, we could not employ men to operate it, and had to do the work in the shot blast room ourselves. At least one of my fellow directors did 4 or 5 hours a week, me doing the balance of 50/60 hours! I was encouraged to go further afield and obtained bed renovations and modernising work from Bath, Chippenham and Devizes as well as Bristol area.

There followed the inevitable showdown with my co-directors, ending in my giving an ultimatum – return my £800 input or I would put the company into receivership – which I was sure I could turn to my advantage and enable me to take it over en-block. It didn't come to that, however as it was agreed to split the company, plant and premises, into 2 halves, one to take over the hospital side and the other the sub contracting side where I had established a sound business manufacturing the filing cabinets I had previously sold!

This was precipitated by a bizarre incident. I had made an appointment to meet two other parties at a London hotel to discuss possible joint purchase of patent rights and outstanding order book of the office equipment company I had worked for who had subsequently gone into liquidation. At the last minute I was forced to cry off to attend to something even more urgent, so arranged for two of the co-director brothers to go in my place.

When they arrived at the office next morning I was all agog to hear what had happened, to be calmly told that they were late starting out, had realised when they reached Newbury that they weren't going to make it, so went to Oxford and spent a pleasant day looking around the colleges! Subsequently I found out the other two parties had met and having decided we/I was not interested, had bought patents and decided to form a new company, using an anagram of their names. This company is still in existence today!

One of the directors whose two brothers formed the remainder of the board asked the third director (the other ex-MOW employee), who had just got married, to join them, making odds of 4 to 1against me. He was the only one who had any financial clout and had already put over £6,000 into the partnership which enabled the formation of the limited company and lost any hope of getting it back. He asked if he could join me, to which I agreed, promising that when we were able we would repay his £6,000 as a first charge. I knew the other directors would want the sub contracting side, this representing 75% of the turnover with hospital side 25%.

I wanted the hospital side as I knew that was where growth was possible, but was equally certain that if I plumped for the hospital side they might smell a rat so I argued for the sub contract side – reluctantly agreeing to take the hospital side after much argument!!

My soon-to-be partner and fellow director John, was in hospital having a quite serious spinal problem attended to, so it fell to me to sort out all the problems of splitting the business into two. Apart from personnel, there was the plant, tooling and materials – and of course premises. Eventually I sorted it all out and on the 1st. October, 1953 a new company was born – HOSPITAL METALCRAFT LTD. I had insisted that, although we could not really afford the money, we established a firm footing for the future. I had given way over premises, taking over by far the worst building, but had previously worked out a plan of action which we could take to make the premises suitable without costing the earth and doing the work ourselves.

My attention to work had been even more stressed when our second son Michael was born in 1951, but this probably toughened my attitude and determination to make a real go of the new project, realising it was a question of 'Did I have it or not?' – entirely up to me!

This had to be done in stages, however, as we needed to earn money right from the start. We opened a new bank account with the national provincial branch in Bedminster, paying in all the money I had left – about £90. As a new entity we had to pay cash for everything before suppliers would release the goods.

One particular item, which was absolutely essential, was oxygen and acetylene gas from BOC. On the first Friday of our new venture I called at the bank, paid in a couple of small cheques and having carefully totted up every penny in our account had just enough to draw the wages of our three employees, duly paid when I got back. I had only just finished entering up our first wages book when the phone went. It was the bank manager wanting to know if I was going to pay in more money that day as we were overdrawn. Disputing this, I immediately drove to the bank taking in my cheque book and the list of all the monies paid. The manager agreed but then pointed out that he had issued me with a cheque book and I had not accounted for the stamps on each cheque! He was right, I had completely forgotten them. He suggested I paid cash from my own pocket to cover the stamps but after a few minutes concentration I said NO you have the cheque book back and I will then be in credit. He agreed but pointed out that I would then have no cheques with which to buy further supplies. Again I agreed, but insisted he took the book and made the necessary entries, then telling him if that was the attitude adopted to someone trying to develop a new business, to keep the account open but I should not be using it as I was sure I could find a more accommodating bank, leaving promptly without shutting the door behind me.

I went straight to the local branch of Midland Bank and after telling the manager exactly what had happened I was able to open an account on the spot with £2 taken from my wallet (leaving me broke!) but in a much happier frame of mind.

The manager was as good as his word and although there were the inevitable hiccups he persevered with us and within months we were able to arrange small overdrafts. We still bank with them. I often wonder what the manager of the National Provincial would think of losing our account – now in the eight figure bracket, and steadily rising!

John gradually resumed work and this proved invaluable as at least he was able to be on the spot and oversee things when I was out selling.

As part of the half and half deal, I had taken over a 1931 Austin Seven and was now able to extend the area I could cover, previously confined to journey by public transport and borrowed cars plus bicycle, ranging as far afield as Gloucester, Taunton, Yeovil and Devizes. I was asked by a hospital at Devizes if we could undertake the modernising of their hospital beds. Without really knowing what was involved, I rashly undertook the job, borrowing a lorry and collecting 30 beds. Without any real knowledge, I bought what I thought were suitable castors and a couple of weeks later borrowed the same lorry to return the beds with the supplies officer quite happy with the result. About 6 months later this had all changed for the worse! Rushing down in my Austin Seven, I soon found out why – the industrial type castors we had fitted were no match for the job they had to do. The supplies officer showing me a sample of the type required which cost about 5 times that of those we had used. He insisted that we replace them at no extra charge, which we eventually did. Fortunately the castor manufacturer making the new castors was prepared to play ball, having been able to satisfy them that we had firm prospects for the future, and let us have the castors on account. So for the following 2/3 months I travelled every week to Devizes taking bed heads and foot ends back after further modifying and fitting new castors. Fortunately we did not have to further treat the bed springs – my little Austin Seven wouldn't have coped with that!

We had further experience of the blinkered tunnel vision of the higher echelon of the Civil Service when we secured work with the then Ministry of Works at their Southwark Bridge London offices. Having successfully completed 3 orders for an item called 'Rack, Head Postmaster' and 'Rack, Post Office Counter', we were given further order on a 'Class A' or similar grading, meaning we did not have to get stage inspection by visiting MOW inspectors, just get on with the job and deliver, possibly with an occasional visit by an inspector if he was in the area. (Not mentioning the numerous times when we would receive a phone call from some other town – an inspector asking how the job was going – and if we received a phone call for him from the London office to say he had been and gone!!)

Having made more than 15,000 of these items over a period of 18 months, we had a further enquiry asking us to quote for a 12,000 batch. With minimal inflation at that time, we quoted the same price as for previous batch of 6,000, at the same time mentioning that we had thought of a way to make the item using modern spot welding technique rather than the pre-war lock-forming method used, and were proposing to take a sample into London office the following week. I duly visited the London office with the proto-type plus quotation for 12,000 batch which showed price of £1.19s.6d each, against £4.2s.0d for older design. Over 50% saving and the item looked and was to all intents and purposes, the same, certainly to the ultimate user.

I was invited into the inner sanctum of the chief executive who, without even looking at the sample, rejected it out of hand. Reason? 'If we were to invite every prospective supplier to submit alternatives to units designed by our experienced team of specialist designers, we would have to go back to grass roots and re-design all our many thousands of items in order to achieve a level playing field.'

I remonstrated, possibly too forcibly, saying that surely such potential massive cost reduction would justify such action, only to politely be shown the door. I didn't get the job for 12,000 of the old design quoted for, learning later from an inspector that we lost the job by ½d – and the firm that did get the order was one where the job had to be inspected at each stage, requiring over 30 visits by inspectors!

I thought then, and still do, it was really a question of keeping his own – and his subordinates' jobs – in fact a classic case of a departmental head having built an empire from the top, the more bodies beneath you, the higher you get. Thus you must do all possible to retain staff, or increase it and fight and reject any proposal which could threaten to reduce numbers.

In particular the retention of the experienced team of designers was very debatable as once firms were invited to tender for supply of goods, they would automatically get their own designers to work to enable them to offer suitable items without merely having to offer items identical to all other bidders and not being able to quote for innovative designs, obviously at no expense to the MOW (except the certainty of lost jobs and staff!).

This also dispensed with the need for inspectors to visit factories all over the UK, jobs being inspected and accepted or rejected when delivered. This dog in the manger attitude was rather reminiscent of the thinking of lower ranks in the army. If a private was given a job of looking after the lavatories and eventually the job needed two men – the first would be made a lance corporal, and if 4 or 5 were ultimately required, the lance corporal could reasonably be expected to be elevated to the lofty position of corporal – with a lance corporal second in command!

The Bristol council decided that at long last they would culvert the stream we had used to wash our beds. The contractors started work and the first thing they did was to build a temporary dam a mile or so upstream to enable them to excavate and lay the necessary large concrete pipes. This job was almost complete when one morning we discovered the dam had burst during the night and our factory was under 3 feet of water! They managed to pump out the flood water later in the day when we faced the daunting task of cleaning up, everything was covered with mud including all the plant – spot welders, presses, even the stove enamelling oven, but most disastrously the home made shot blasting plant where all the shot grit used had to be literally dug up and scrapped, only managing to save the bare chamber and hoses. All the jobs in hand had to be hand washed before we could complete them, having to get them sprayed within hours before they rusted up completely. We received a visit from the contractor's insurers who told us to put in our claim which would receive urgent and sympathetic attention. We did so, rather nervously putting in a claim for just over £400 which was paid out on the spot, discovering later that had this claim been for £5,000 it would have been settled equally quickly!

We made a real break-through when a local hospital favoured us with an order for 60 medicine cabinets to replace their existing clapped out wooden cupboards with metal units, made to similar style and dimensions. Encouraged by this, I ventured on our first mailing shot, having single sheet (very poor quality paper) leaflets with a line drawing of the cabinet.

We sent out several hundred, getting the addresses from the telephone directories and addressing the envelopes by hand (I had to do something when I got home in the evenings!) and wife and boys became quite good at stuffing and stamping envelopes!

These efforts and personal calls with sample cabinets enabled us to sell over 1,500 in the first 3/4 months. Yet the cabinets were very basic and of very poor quality as good sheet metal was very difficult to obtain unless one ordered 8 or 10 tons at a time. This encouraged us to spread our wings ever further, increasing both area and range of items offered.

When the first British Standard Medicine/Poison Cupboards Standard was introduced in 1958 we decided to completely re-design (and scrap) our first venture in this direction, which we thought had done so well, and make an entirely new range of cabinets of very good quality.

We took a small stand at the first hospital equipment exhibition to be held in London after the war, with totally unexpected success. Several other manufacturers had their versions on show, but we had decided to forget price and go for quality and as a result we were inundated with orders. All hospitals had been ordered to bring their storage systems into line with the new British Standard. Apart from taking orders for several hundred cabinets we were approached on the stand by the managing director of a long established hospital equipment manufacturing firm with a huge catalogue, including beds, who persuaded us to allow them, through their 40 plus area salesmen to handle these cabinets, with us also selling direct. Terms were agreed, minimum batch sizes of 10 of each model (6 models) delivery to their Birmingham area stores, 17½% discount, payment up front! We were quite happy with this and their first order for 12 cabinets, 2 of each went smoothly. At that time we were receiving orders for 30, 40, 50 cabinets at a time from hospitals all over the UK, and quoting for equally large batches to hospitals without hearing further from them.

I thought at the time that hospitals had been unable to get necessary funding. Cold calling at a Derbyshire hospital, the pharmacy staff rather surprisingly said the chief pharmacist wanted to see me. This was one of the hospitals I had unsuccessfully quoted some 3–4 months previously (I always made sure of researching quotes etc. whenever I was on the road – thus knew my facts) so thought I was to be given the order.

Exactly the opposite – I was greeted most rudely and berated for exhibiting cabinets made to a high standard and supplying junk. Showing him my quotation I pointed out they had not even ordered cabinets from us. Whereupon he produced his copy of his order, giving full specification of 75 Bristol Maid cabinets (our adopted trade name) showing full details and prices. I pointed out the order was not made out to us, but to the other firm acting as our agents, but also telling him that his order alone was more than the total sold to the named company. They had simply taken one each of our cabinets to a local sheet metal works and had them copied! Obviously at much lower prices than our discounted cabinets – especially for such very inferior units. The pharmacist was convinced that we had made the cabinets he had purchased and took me down to a ward. From 50 feet away I could see they were not ours and pointed out numerous faults from yards away. All he could do, as all the cabinets were fitted to the walls and in use, was to agree to write to the firm involved, asking for redress and threatening never to use them again. Apparently this was widely taken up by other hospitals similarly duped. Certainly within a matter of 5/6 years this very long established firm went out of business – but not before I had learnt another lesson the hard way!

We had always wanted to live in the country, which we did when the success of the company allowed us to purchase a bungalow at Failand, about 3 miles from our works, but beautifully sited in a country setting. It was still not entirely to my liking (and certainly not to my wife's) and my first job was to replace the black bathroom suite! This had probably put off the opposition when we bought the property! This was followed up by adding a big kitchen extension then knocking down the small lean to garage and building a much larger one. I had moved on from the Austin Seven and my second hand Humber Snipe wouldn't allow me to open the door when the car was in the garage! I did all the work myself, but was stumped when it came to felting the flat roof. However, an employee of some 3 months standing heard that I was looking for a flat roof felter and said his father-in-law was experienced in this type of work. I arranged for necessary materials to be delivered, took both to the site one Saturday morning and left them to get on with it. Returning at about 5.00p.m., I was horrified at what they had done! I should have expected it, they were both Irish, but I completely lost my temper. I chucked them both off the site telling them I didn't have time to take them back as I had to get to work and strip off all the felt they had laid before the tar set. My parting words were, 'Don't expect me to pay either of you for this,' and to my employee, 'And don't you bother coming to work on Monday, I'll post your cards on to you,' which I did with absolute minimum of delay! Glad said she had never seen me so angry!

Our landlord had a big area of land on which he was selling plots for factories and we agreed to buy a plot about 100ft × 350ft. At that time we were making a range of chassis for electrical products for a local electronics manufacturer, this being a job we had tooled-up and which fitted in very well with our other activities, filling in otherwise void periods in our works. The owner learnt of our purchase and approached our landlord to see if he could buy a site alongside ours. There was only a narrow strip about 25 ft wide remaining, this having originally been allocated for an access road, but due to change of plans this was now not needed. It was agreed that this should be added to our site, thereby increasing the width to 125ft, still not sufficient for 2 factories and 2 access roads so we drew up and submitted plans showing a factory on either side of a 25ft wide shared access road, this also to house all main services including drains for both units, only to be told by the planning authorities that the other party involved had submitted plans which had been approved, showing his factory 12" away from the dividing central line and his own much narrower service road on the other side of the building. This left us with no alternative but to re-submit our plans with our building backing onto theirs, and with an equally narrow service road.

Another lesson learnt the hard way – as from the day we agreed the original deal, we didn't receive a further order for the chassis, rendering the special tooling scrap!

There was a very active pensioner, a retired builder, living in a caravan near our site and as we planned to do most of the building of the new works ourselves, he was pleased to be called in to start the project off, pegging out the site levels and footings and to do the bricklaying once we had put in the footings. He laid out the levels (and site) without using modern levelling instruments. A real eye opener – using a coil of hose pipe he tied one end to a stake at the front of the site, then filling the hose with water at the rear of the site, lowered the filled hose until the water stopped flowing, making the site level! 100% correct as later proved by the building inspector who passed it without query!

The builder had only laid 7 or 8 courses of bricks when he died suddenly. I carried on building the inside walls, putting in toilet drains and then found another bricklayer who did the outside work, not being proficient or confident enough to undertake that work myself! We put on the roof ourselves with help from a couple of workers in the factory who wanted the overtime as the normal day's work had to be kept going to ensure cash flow was maintained.

We moved in and within 12 months realised that even more space was required, resulting in our building over the rest of our site with a 60ft wide × 150ft long building, subcontracting the main work but again doing footings, floor and drains ourselves to keep costs down! Our building activities were restricted to a few hours during the week if I was not on the road, and weekends, including Fridays which was a NO–GO day as far as hospital visits were concerned.

My co-director, John used to take his full share of this building work, but seemed to lose enthusiasm and interest in the business itself, especially when he got heavily involved in boating, later moving on to power boating, when the business was very much put on the back burner, with numerous associated costs falling on the business.

My son Brian joined us at the factory, becoming very proficient in all phases of the work involved, sheet metal, welding, tool-making and we lent him to an associated business to start filing cabinet manufacture for several months, bringing him back when it became obvious the other staff in that set up were being totally uncooperative and hostile towards him – but taking full advantage of his output and expertise!

When Brian married, we looked around and bought a semi-detached house at Backwell, then under a council closing order as it was deemed uninhabitable. Which it most certainly was! A young couple with a baby living there were emigrating to Australia. When we took possession having obtained necessary permits to re-build, we found plastic fertiliser bags held in position by flattened corn flake cartons nailed up to the ceiling inside the rooms upstairs to keep the rain off both their bed and the baby's cot!

The first job was to strip off the roof. What better day to do this than Christmas Day – which didn't exactly please the couple of middle aged ladies living next door! We raised the walls, put on a new tiled roof, replaced the narrow stairs leading off the front room with open plan stairs, new windows, doors, built a very large new kitchen, hall, bathroom, toilet onto rear of house and in doing so had to open up a window to create a new door into the kitchen. As with all old cottages the wall was about 22" wide at the foundation level, tapering to 12" at eaves height. We had to cut a 36" long 20" wide × 24" high solid stone block in half to make room for the door and succeeded, at the expense of completely splitting my right arm

VERY FEW ROSES – EVEN LESS HONEY!

muscle in two – as well as the stone – since when I have lost all strength in that arm. On investigating the so-called cesspit which took all foul drainage (including toilets) from both houses, we found it was 30" x 30" x 30" deep and had been overflowing for years into a ditch running alongside the adjacent hedge. We built a new septic tank, 20' x 8' x 8' deep at the bottom end of the garden, having obtained construction details from local library. It was a very wet, low lying area, no JCBs in those days, and they would not have been able to get it to site had there been, it was a case of hand digging, finding our excavation completely filled with water every time we returned to carry on digging and having to spend a couple of hours baling out before being able to start digging again. The resultant septic tank was very successful, it never requiring to be emptied. Next door neighbours declined our offer to connect them for a modest sum, instead spent many hundreds of pounds having a cesspit built, which had to be emptied every 6 months or so!

I was travelling widely, visiting Ireland and Scotland for week long stints 4 or 5 times a year. I established very sound connections which have endured and grown to the degree that visits now have to be made monthly to both areas. I used to let enquires build up until I could visit 5 or 6 hospitals on one journey. Remembering one such day trip, I made appointments starting at Blackburn for 8.00a.m. then onto Huddersfield, Leeds (Jimmy's), Wakefield, Nottingham and Derby – where I realised I was not going to make the 4.00p.m. appointment at Leicester. I phoned up the supplies officer at Leicester who agreed to wait for me until 6.30p.m. I made the appointment, then travelled back to Bristol in my second hand Humber estate car, as usual calling in at the factory around midnight to find a message on my desk saying an appointment had been made for me at Guys Hospital at 8.30a.m. next morning where the new tower block was being built. I made that appointment, followed by many others as we did a lot of work for the new hospital, including designing many new items of equipment.

During the early days of the company, I was approached several times by 'dodgy' hospital officials wanting to horn-in on our success. When I was visiting one hospital, whilst doing my usual spiel, the supplies officer was called away but before he left the office he handed me the hospital accounts covering the previous year. After 15/20 minutes he returned, asking if I had found them interesting, then drawing my attention to the section showing he had spent some 2 million pounds – and this was many, many years ago. He carried on by saying that over half of this sum could be spent through my company! Then elaborated by saying that I wouldn't have to do anything – he would arrange orders, contracts etc. We would issue the orders, to the suppliers after receiving hospital orders, goods would be sent direct, us to follow up with invoices, payments etc., us adding 2½% for our trouble. He said he was sure we could find room for a sleeping director. Diplomatically (I thought) I declined any interest in such a project, he promptly closed the interview, with the parting comment 'Close the door behind you and don't bother to call on me again.' It was not until after he retired that we received further orders from that hospital.

Another learning curve for myself was when a supplies officer submitted a professional third angle projection drawing of a special trolley he wanted. This included all details down to BSS weld specifications, bend radius etc, and projected loading which was only a few pounds. I rang him to say I thought the construction was totally inadequate, only to be instructed to quote to the drawing or not expect further work from his hospital. I quoted but took care to increase the gauge of tube etc., (which he wouldn't be able to check) and finally ended the quotation by saying we suspected the design was too flimsy.

We received the order and duly made and delivered this trolley late one afternoon. At 9.00a.m. the next morning I had a phone call from his office saying the trolley had failed its first test and instructing me to visit him immediately!! I jumped into my car and called into the kitchen where the trolley had been delivered, to be confronted by a very sad looking trolley with broken back – the centre of the trolley was bent down and touching the ground!

I learnt that this trolley had been purchased to transport empty bakers trays (used for carrying cakes) back to the kitchen from the dining room, with a load of about 14/15 lbs. Just before the kitchen closed the previous day a 10 ton load of potatoes had arrived – what better means of transporting them to the stores than on this brand new trolley! Which was promptly loaded with about 20 x 1cwt sacks. Eventually I was confronted by the supplies officer, who insisted that we repaired the trolley or else! We did so, re-designing as necessary, at our own cost.

Lesson learnt – never let your own judgement be over-ridden by amateurs, even paid ones, since then we have always tried to persuade potential customers to our way of thinking, if unsuccessful, adding date to the price to ensure the order was not placed, and if it was, we should make sufficient profit to offset any subsequent costs should we be called to task in the future.

In 1962 a couple of business associates persuaded me to take up golf, and I joined Knowle Golf club. I couldn't really spare the time and actually paid subscriptions for 2 years without even visiting the club. Then I started playing evenings and the occasional Sunday morning. I progressed reasonably well, although I was not one who took easily to lessons and after a couple of short sessions the club professional told me, in no uncertain Scottish language 'to do it my way, or take up bowls!!'

Finding myself free one Saturday afternoon, I went down with the intention of going to the practice field, only to be invited to join them by 3 players waiting to play, despite me telling them I was a total beginner. I found out they were the club captain, chairman and secretary. Walking off the final green, the secretary looked at the captain saying, 'Well, what handicap shall I give him?' and after further discussion with the chairman they agreed on 20, when I would have been pleased had they said 24!

This encouraged me to try and play more often, but I never managed more than twice a week, and this only because I picked up with a couple of chaps who worked nights, and we had many rounds starting about 6.15a.m., after they had finished work (not at a very physically demanding job), me then going on to work until 8.00 or 9.00p.m. I soon found a considerable number of golfing pals, most of whom were established golfers, including my sponsors who were both single figure golfers, as were numerous of the others. After a couple of years, one of my pals, a jeweller received an invite to play in a company match in Scotland and asked me if I would like to join him with another of the players, if he could arrange invites. He did and we did, me arranging to make a long promised visit to three hospitals in Edinburgh, possibly having been asked to join them as I had a big Humber estate car, well able to carry all the golf clubs and trolleys! This started a very long friendship which still sees us playing together every Wednesday over 30 years later.

I relate the above as it threw up a remarkable coincidence. After driving to Scotland on the Sunday and playing 18 holes on the course being used for the competition – No. 1 Gullane – plus a further 12 holes at Galashiels, curtailed by rain, we booked in at our Edinburgh hotel at 7.00p.m. then went to another hotel where our host had invited us to meet all the players and their wives for a meal and get together, including arranging order of play on the Tuesday following. When I was introduced to my playing partner, I found out he came from Penzance, so I mentioned that a great pal called Matthews who had been killed during the war also came from there. Whereupon he said, 'Wait a minute whilst I introduce you to my wife.' He called her over, introduced me and then asked me to carry on what I was saying about 'Math'. She then revealed that she was Math's sister! She had been little more than a baby when he was killed, and I spent several hours over the next few days talking about those times spent at Frome, St. Albans and Kent.

I spent Monday calling at hospitals as arranged, the tournament was on the Tuesday, without success, then back to Bristol the next day, playing 18 holes at Cheltenham on the way!

For the first 15–18 years of the company we bought very little new plant, scouring engineering auctions to pick up second hand plant at a fraction of the new price. When needing a much larger capacity air compressor, we attended an auction in North London, and bought two compressors lumped in a single lot for £260. We kept the larger unit and sold the small unit after advertising it in a second hand machinery magazine for £400. Allowing £140 for cost of transporting both items to Bristol, we obtained the compressor we wanted for nothing. On another occasion, attending an auction in Bristol we were looking for some heavy racking to hold heavy tools in. We inspected those on offer, discovered in the auction room that several other unsold lots had been lumped with the one we wanted, no one else bid and our first bid of £10 was accepted. Which meant we had bought not only the racks we wanted but 20 or so very heavy steel tables and trolleys weighing over 6 tons which cost us nearly £20 to get transported to our works, all are still in daily use some 30 years plus later!

Life was further complicated as I was really not able to entrust John to do any job with any real confidence, as evidenced when a large quantity of steel tube, nearly 50,000 feet of the type we were regularly having to buy, went under the hammer when a business only a couple of miles away was sold up. At the last minute on the morning of the auction I had to visit a hospital on business, entrusting John with the task of attending the auction, knowing for a certainty that there would be very few, if any, other people interested in this lot.

It was worth between £600–£700. John confessed next morning that he had gone out for a cup of tea, not expecting the lot to come up for another hour, finding when he came back that it had been bought by a farmer for £18. Not prepared to lose it as easily as that, I went out to the works to be told the farmer had collected it with a tractor the previous afternoon. I found out where his farm was, about 12 miles away and went straight there, to find he had dumped it all in a barn with his straw stock. He told me he had a job where he wanted about 1,000 feet, bid what that would have cost him and found the whole lot knocked down to him. I offered £120 for the surplus, approximately 49,000ft., us to move it, he jumped at the chance, giving him the tube he wanted and £100 as well. For months afterwards our factory was littered with straw as the oily tube seemed to attract every little bit of chaff and straw within reach when we collected it.

I really had very little time for holidays with the family, but Glad pressurised me to take a week off on holiday in a caravan (any site had to be properly serviced with running water, flush toilet and electricity of course!), and this grew to two weeks, usually spent in Devon and Cornwall for a few years until the boys persuaded me (and Glad first of all) to go camping.

I bought a couple of ridge tents and a large fly sheet which we used to set up spanning both tents, thus creating space for a table and primus in the middle. We then used to get away for weekends usually late on Friday, returning late Sunday, and this quickly superseded the caravan holidays. Even when it rained the whole time we were 'on holiday'!

One year we went to Spain, camping out on the way there and back, the only upset being when in company with another 40 or so campers, we had to pack up and leave the camp in the middle of the night when we found the site was overrun by millions of ants!

This resulted in us having to change all our clothes and shake out all our bedding and spare clothes, plus the interior of the car and the camping gear as soon as we reached a field offering a degree of privacy when morning came.

To be nearer my work, we bought a house at South Liberty Lane, a pre-war terrace type, and not long after moving there my youngest son Michael was born.

The house had a very small kitchen with back door leading directly onto a narrow garden, which flooded at the slightest sign of rain. There was a small outside coal house, so I decided to pull this down, build an extension to house the sink, cooker etc., with back door leading off this, the effect being to increase the size of the kitchen enormously. I also built an outside toilet at the end of the kitchen extension.

When I took over the Austin Seven, there was no garage, but I could park it at the back where there was a hard standing drive-way to the rear of all the houses.

On my way to work one day, council workers had started work to re-align the road beneath a railway bridge. I asked the foreman where he was disposing of the very good topsoil they had to move, and he was delighted when I said he could tip it on my back garden, 300 yards away, instead of taking it as intended to a tip 6 miles away.

So I got home to find about 60 tons of soil awaiting my attention. Also about 20 tons of old paving stones and other hardcore! This soil raised the level of my garden by over a foot and the hardcore and paving stones soon found themselves used as a base for garage and garden path, with enough paving stones remaining to enable me to pave the front garden and create small low level paved garden plots – still in being to this day!

I obtained sufficient second hand timber and flat asbestos sheet to make a 9ft x 16ft garage at the back, with felt roofing on wood obtained from old tobacco crates (3d each – 4 required – total cost of garage less than £10!) Plus a lot of sweat!

Money was still at a premium; every penny we could spare after paying John back the money he had lost in his previous venture was ploughed back into the business. I did make quite a reasonable profit when I sold 5 or 6 houses after renovating them, except the once when I needed the profit to start the business and moved to a cheaper house.

The one thing I would not countenance was buying orders. Not long after starting the business I had to collect a punch tool from a small firm specialising in this type of work. I called as requested at 6.00p.m. one evening to find the job only just started and it would take another couple of hours. The owner said it was pay night and asked me to join him on a sort of pub crawl. We visited 4 or 5 pubs, at each buying half a pint, then he would meet a man and make a bee line for the toilet, returning after a couple of minutes. He eventually told me these chaps all worked at BAC (the Bristol Aeroplane Company), his previous employer, and channelled work to him. This was when he paid them for their efforts, anything from £10 to £25 depending on the value of the job obtained. A few years later BAC cancelled a projected new engine, all this work stopped, and he had to cut his workforce from 35 to 4 in one fell swoop!

The only occasion I ever strayed from my decision not to do this was entirely inadvertently, when calling at a major London hospital at the request of a very senior official. After completing our business he said, 'Time for lunch – come to my club with me.' After a good meal with wine in his very posh club, when the bill was brought to the table he got up and said, 'See you in a minute' and disappeared into the toilet, obviously leaving me to settle up! He never caught me like that again. He later rose to one of the top jobs in the Ministry, and although I frequently saw him many times at exhibitions and other meetings when he was in the chair or main speaker, he totally ignored me!

Having been schooled in the Christmas habit of giving our customers in the engineering sector a bottle or two at Christmas, I bought a dozen bottles of whisky and did the rounds of my new hospital clients, returning with my 12 bottles intact, all having been refused, even though I offered them as raffle prizes at their Christmas parties! So my staff received unexpected Christmas presents that year – as did John and myself, even though we couldn't afford it!

When we had a spell of very heavy orders for a quite straightforward job, which we were too busy to handle, we tried sub-contracting the item to a friend doing similar work. After 5 or 6 weeks waiting for the job to materialise, with our hospital customers chasing us for the items we had been promised within 10/14 days, we had a first delivery, which we rejected out of hand due to their very poor quality. We had to work very extended hours doing the job ourselves, losing both money and a so called friend at the same time, but learning that if we wanted a good job there was no alternative but to do it ourselves. We have never since sub-contracted any job we were capable of doing in our own works.

Years later when we first made examination couches and didn't have the necessary know-how or plant to carry out the upholstery, we did buy out for a time, but took on the job ourselves when we found that deadlines for delivery were not being met. We set up our own upholstery department, and have never regretted this decision.

Eventually we decided to move into stainless steel, first doing sheet metal items, eventually graduating to the much more difficult but rewarding tubular steel products.

Always having been aware that the real strength of any business was the element of goodwill it enjoyed, I found this so on numerous occasions. Every business makes mistakes and we were no exception, totally misinterpreting what was required on one order, and being told so in no uncertain terms by the receiving hospital on the same day as the goods were delivered. We put in hand immediately the correct item and delivered the following afternoon, collecting the faulty trolleys. We received due acknowledgement of our actions, but for months afterwards we were hearing tales of our prompt remedial action, being recounted at area and regional meetings of supplies officers!

The value of goodwill was never more clearly illustrated than when I received a phone call from a supplies officer at Gloucester, with whom we had established a very good relationship. After some ten minutes of conversation, 'How is the family?' 'Where are you going for your holiday?' 'How is the car going?' etc., etc., I gently asked what we could do for him.

His reply, 'We have just started to renovate a theatre, didn't know what to do with all the equipment, much of which could do with refurbishing, so have loaded it all onto a furniture van which is on its way to you. Do whatever you think is required, dropping me a line before you send it back (within 3 weeks please) and I will let you have covering order'. Obviously there was no way we were going to overcharge or say we had done work which we hadn't, he finished up getting a better deal than if correct procedures had been followed!

We had an arrangement with a hospital in the Forest of Dean to upgrade all their beds, but as they could only spare two at a time we arranged to divert a van into the area when possible after advising them by phone to get a further two beds ready. This both reduced transport charge and spread the cost over a longer period. The supplies officer in Gloucester would raise a covering order when we submitted our invoice, usually at 4 to 5 week intervals. Halfway through this job the supplies officer retired.

When the new supplies officer received our invoice he rang

me for an explanation, then responded by saying he was not going to raise a covering order and had no intention of paying and would be returning our invoice. It took nearly 18 months for him to raise an order and pass our invoice for payment, and we never completed renovating the hospital beds!

Some time later we were requested to visit a hospital at Tetbury, also within his area, and quote for repairing the spring mattress on one bed. I knew exactly what was required, so quoted to collect, repair and return, which added up to about twice the cost of a new bed. He rejected my quote, when I couldn't resist telling him that when similar work was previously required, I had put them in touch with a bicycle shop a few hundred yards from the hospital who had sent someone round with suitable tools, charging them 15/– when the job was completed, which is all we would have done anyway!

Subsequently, several times we sent out, knowingly, incorrect items when correct items were not quite ready, phoning the recipient hospital telling them the wrong trolleys had been loaded and to refuse delivery, sending the correct trolleys the next day, when we had found time to finish them, adding enormously to our goodwill!

I had also learnt, particularly when working for the office equipment firm, of the vital importance of keeping readily available records of what had been supplied. The only recourse then had been to refer back to invoice copies, not readily available and frequently not sufficiently detailed. A doctor would ring up and order another 6 cabinets to add to those he had purchased a year previously. The order would be sent forward to our stores, requiring them to return same to the supplies office asking for a cabinet model, finish colour etc., often resulting in the office guessing what was required, and an indignant doctor ringing up saying he was not going to pay his account until we had supplied cream cabinets to replace the green ones delivered, and he proposed to deduct a sum of money when he did pay to offset the inconvenience factor, and this could very well be in Newcastle or Liverpool etc.!!!

From day one, I recorded every order when completed, these showing full details of transactions which would be necessary to enable repeat orders to be correctly fulfilled at any future date. This came to be regarded as our Bible and has been maintained ever since – often surprising phone callers when asked to requote for items supplied many years previously by giving required details in 10–20 seconds! Even computers now used would NOT have records going back 25–30 years!

The annual exhibition in London, eventually held every other year, proved invaluable to us. When we first started, matrons governed every factor within the hospital, frequently her husband was secretary or supplies officer, both them and staff being wedded to their work – it being regarded as a vocation rather than a job of work. Once confidence was established with the matron, you were given carte blanche to call on anyone in the hospital who required new equipment, obviously funnelling back any quotes to matron or the secretary. This direct access and contact vanished with the matrons, hence the visit of hospital staff, particularly theatre and sterile supplies personnel, to our stand was the one opportunity given of making contact with them and getting their reaction to our products and ideas. We therefore made a real sustained effort to ensure that we had items on our stand which were totally new, not always ideal or what was wanted, but at least it gave us the opportunity of obtaining the views of our visitors, both constructive and more importantly destructive, the latter being far more useful in my view.

Returning to the progress and development of Hospital Metalcraft, about 5–6 years after commencing business I received a phone call from a matron of a local hospital asking if we made medicine trolleys. Replying honestly that I didn't even know what such a trolley was, she replied that she had ordered one which was advertised by a national company, which was totally useless. It was a cupboard mounted on a tubular frame fitted with castors, completely unstable and she had consigned it to the outside yard and was refusing to use it! I arranged to visit and discuss, then spent many hours watching the methods being used, and after much questioning of ward and pharmacy staff I returned to the factory and produced a prototype of what I felt would best do the job. Within a week I took this medicine trolley to the hospital for evaluation. Everyone was wildly enthusiastic, and put it into immediate use and within a couple of weeks we had quoted and received orders for some 20 plus for that hospital.

This was the only occasion I can remember when we hit the jackpot with the first prototype. About 10 years ago we were asked to collect and recondition this very first trolley – which we were pleased to do without charge, and as far as I know it is still in use today!

When this trolley was shown at the next International Medical Exhibition at Olympia, we were inundated with orders, since when we have certainly made well over 200,000 of this and similar models, offered in laminate versions as well as the original sheet metal design, and they continue to be regularly supplied to hospitals abroad as well as in the UK.

We moved from South Liberty Lane after several years when profit generated from the sale allowed us to move to a larger house off Clifton Downs. Immediately we set about improving this – including building an indoors downstairs toilet, this work being completed just in time to allow me to sell it quickly, at a reasonable profit. I had to sell in order to raise the capital necessary when I decided to split from former company and join John in establishing Hospital Metalcraft Ltd., realising something less than £1,000, but it has certainly paid off. The small terraced property I bought in Bedminster again allowed me to use my DIY talents, rapidly improving it by adding a new bathroom and toilet, which turned out to be a major task. I also removed the chimney and chimney breast one brick at a time (working from a ladder) and dropping them down the chimney before taking them through the house into the front garden. The resulting mess did not make me the flavour of the month with my wife, especially as work was delayed when I caught mumps! I made a further modest profit when I moved to a relatively new semi-detached house much closer to my factory.

There was a sequel to the above – one of my next door neighbours complained to the council (not directly to me) that by raising the level of my garden, I had caused his to flood. A building inspector was called in, pointed out a few facts and the complaint was totally rejected.

This neighbour also complained that he had a long established pigeon loft in his garden and cats could climb on my garage roof and jump onto the roof of his loft. He was told to put up some wire netting on the side facing my garage or move his loft.

All of this was not conducive to good relationship between neighbours! However, the neighbour on the other side remained the best of friends and I later arranged for a few loads of soil to be dumped on his garden, a similar offer having been refused by the dissenting neighbour!

In 1969 it became apparent that we required more

141

accommodation, and as we could not find a site in Bristol, which at first seemed the obvious solution as it would enable us to keep our existing workforce, we decided to look further afield. At that time the Board of Trade rigidly controlled the issue of LDT (Land Development Certificates) and when we approached them they wanted us to relocate to the far North East (Jarrow or Tyneside) or West Wales (Swansea or the Rhondda) being suggested. This was certainly not acceptable to us, so we scoured Somerset and Dorset, being unwilling to move too far from our roots in Bristol.

At a site at Sherborne we were told we would not be welcome there as we were classed as industrial with unacceptable metal treatment processes! Shaftesbury welcomed us but were not forthcoming with site or terms when we got down to the nitty gritty, and then there was Weymouth, the old Whitehead Torpedo works which looked most promising. Returning to the Board of Trade in Bristol we were told that as this site already was designated for light engineering, they couldn't stop us from moving there, but if we did they would have to revoke our existing certificate on our Bristol site! This made it impossible to proceed further with that site and we looked around further. Sites at the old stations of Templecombe and Stalbridge were stalled when British Rail procrastinated and it was impossible to get anyone to make a decision.

When attending the Annual Dorset Regiment Reunion Dinner at Dorchester, an old army pal from Blandford told me that he thought there were plots available on an allotment site at Blandford. We investigated immediately and within a few weeks had contracted to buy an acre plot on the site now occupied, later buying a further 1½ acres adjoining.

Back to the Board of Trade, who said we would not be

allowed to build more than 5,000 square feet, without losing our certificate at Bristol, so that was that! We built a factory 4,990sq.ft. including a small office area, my elder son Brian agreeing to move with his wife and small son to Blandford to start operations. At first, this involved manufacture of tubular trolley frames of all types, and having no treatment facilities at Blandford, we arranged with a local firm to deliver these frames to our Bristol works for finishing and assembly.

Business was thriving and we really needed to expand this factory, but again the Board of Trade blocked every approach. After receiving a large number of export enquires at the Olympia Exhibition, we reapplied, listing same and saying both factories were bursting at the seams, also saying that if we were still refused permission to expand, we would be taking it up with our local MPs at Dorset and in Bristol. They said they would be sending men down to make an on the spot inspection. They duly arrived at a time when the factory was filled to the eaves and literally hundreds of frames were stacked outside ready for collection later that day, although I omitted to mention that.

They said we had obviously built up our stock anticipating their arrival, then left to go direct to Bristol works, which they found equally full. Two or three weeks later we received permission to build a further 10,000sq.ft. at Blandford, and we put this in hand, only to find that before we had even completed that extension all requirements to obtain development certificates were abolished, so we added a further 20,000sq.ft. making a total of about 30,000sq.ft.

What has never ceased to surprise me is the total lack of assistance proffered both by national and local government bodies. In 30 years the only correspondence ever received from the local council had been to acknowledge receipt of our letters requesting information – never any response to queries!

In 1970 we decided our long term future would be in Blandford and I moved to live in Broadstone, following John's move a few years previously. Brian was gradually building up both staff and plant including shot blast and finishing facilities. John, supposedly was in attendance daily, but actually turned up for a few hours 2 or 3 times a week. I commuted to Bristol three sometimes four days a week, filling in at Blandford on other days.

When the decision was taken to move the company to Blandford, John also decided to move to Poole, buying a house with long frontage to Poole harbour complete with small boat house and landing stage. The main object as far as I was concerned was that he would be on site to oversee building of the first phase of the factory, an 'at cost' agricultural concrete span building fronted by small office and toilet block. It turned out later that this work, carried out by a boating friend of John's who later moved to Canada, was very unsatisfactory as far as the office block was concerned, footings being totally inadequate, resulting in the whole block ultimately having to be replaced.

When Brian was firmly settled at the new Blandford factory and had bought a bungalow locally he engaged and trained new staff, first to manufacture tubular steel trolleys, and when the new extension was built, covering all aspects, sheet metal plus pre-treatment/degreasing, epoxy resin powder coating, shot blasting etc., with the intention that by the time we closed down Bristol, Blandford could cope with all work involved, including stainless steel, laminate wood and upholstery.

When we decided to move our home to Dorset. I must admit my choice of area was greatly influenced by its proximity to the prestigious Broadstone Golf Club where after 5 years I was elected to the committee and spent upwards of 5 years as chairman of the green, development committee and deputy chairman of the club. Subsequently I was invited to become captain which I declined as it would have taken up too much of my time.

After moving to Broadstone, for over 10 years I divided my time between the two factories, commuting to Bristol every Monday, Wednesday and Thursday – Tuesdays, Fridays and Saturdays at Blandford. I used to leave home for Bristol at about 5.00a.m., and must admit I used to thoroughly enjoy the early morning journeys, wild life in abundance and beautiful sunrises (plus rain, fog and snow on occasions!)

My younger son, Michael, worked for about a year with Frys at Keynsham, after leaving university, then joining us at the Bristol works, always with the intention of moving to Blandford, which he did when we closed the Bristol works and made all staff redundant. We offered jobs at Blandford to all, including relocation costs, but only one person took this up, one of our longest serving men, but even he did not move house. He commuted daily from Keynsham, about 50 miles each way, until retiring some 16 years later.

Shortly after this, relationships with my fellow director became very strained. John was an extremely likeable and straightforward chap, but seemed to have lost all interest in the company, certainly his input compared to mine could be rated on a scale of 5% to 95% – plus the fact that my two sons, although not directors and having no financial/shares interest, were putting in a tremendous amount of effort for their weekly wage packets. John and myself, as the company shares were divided equally between us, continued to draw identical wages. John had received many more perks than I, bits and pieces for houses, including labour both by workers and outside tradesmen, and numerous transport and labour costs involving his boats and associated interests.

Direct negotiations spread over several years proved fruitless, and all the time the company continued to grow impressively, with yearly sales increasing by between 10% and 20% without being influenced by John in any way. Despite consulting the company auditors, an internationally renowned firm, and incurring personal expenses approaching £2,000, we received no concrete advice. 'We have to advise that in cases like this direct negotiations between you and your fellow director are the only means of arriving at any type of settlement.' I eventually agreed an arrangement paying a large sum of cash, 5 years service agreement, fixed annual salary for doing nothing, plus car, pension payments in exchange for John's shares.

This remained the position for several years, finally coming to a head when John wanted further cash for a project he was involved in, so enabling me to more or less dictate the terms, a single cash payment plus terminating all other perks. At long last I owned the entire company, enabling me to immediately transfer John's shares to my sons, making them directors and so rewarding them for their involvement and efforts over many years. When I lost my wife, who had been allocated shares many years previously, I then transferred all our shares equally to Brian and Michael and their families.

In the following years I took every opportunity of taking golfing holidays in Scotland and in the North of England, usually with 3 other golfers, combining business with pleasure. I called at hospitals in the morning, played golf in the afternoon and evening! Eventually I joined the club professional and 10 or so others on golfing holidays on the continent, always in February, when it did not interfere too much with work! On the final day of our first holiday in Spain we all had lunch in a swish restaurant, lobster, king prawns, the lot! Only one member expressed a wish for a sweet and ordered a gateaux, whereupon the waiter produced a side table with large carving knife and fork. Bill took some ribbing – 'All for a slice of cake!' The waiter duly returned with a huge covered tureen which he placed on the table – whipped off the lid pronouncing 'El Gato, senor.' El Gato being the restaurant's tom cat! A real Spanish sense of humour! Bill never did get his cake but we at least gained a name for our golfing society 'El Gato' and a tie illustrating same.

Of many memorable happenings one to be forgotten is when I arrived at Lisbon to find after a phone call home that I had left my passport on the sideboard! I had to spend a few hours under lock and key in the airport police station whilst the pro and another pal contacted the British Consul (out playing tennis on a Sunday afternoon) and eventually had me freed after standing guarantor – me having to visit the consulate and get a temporary passport first thing on the Monday morning!

Camping was losing its appeal, particularly in the Cornwall area where we seemed to take rain and bad weather with us on every trip. We took holidays in hotels and became regulars at a hotel in Falmouth where we became good friends with the owners and played regularly on the local Falmouth Golf Course. A few weeks after returning from such a holiday, my friend phoned to tell me the owner of the course had died and the course would probably be put up for sale.

Although business was thriving, my wife, family and myself were only too conscious of the fact that my contribution was at least 80% to John's 20% and after weighing up all the pros and cons and finance factors, I decided to see if I could buy the course. My son and I with minimal outside help could look after the course with Brian's wife and Glad, again with our part time help, running the club house. My solicitor was quite excited: 'Never bought a golf course!' but after several months the family of the deceased owner decided not to sell, possibly the hand of fate again!

During one of our golfing holidays in Spain I discussed the possibility of buying a building plot on offer around a new golf course near Marbella, when the cost of a plot and building a superb bungalow would have been less than £8,000 which I and a very close pal would buy jointly. On our return home, discussing it with my wife, I had to drop the idea because Glad flatly refused to fly and no way was I prepared to waste three or four weeks a year driving there and back! These properties now fetch upwards of £300,000.

Subsequently, I bought 5 weeks timeshare at the St.Mellion club in Cornwall, where my family and friends, plus some of our works staff spent many happy holidays. Four weeks were during the summer, with one week in autumn reserved for golfing friends only! I felt justified in taking up these timeshares, as being on lease only they would pass to my children free of death duties in due course. A few years after I bought the government moved the goal posts and no such duties would have been levied anyway!

Whilst always a keen player of golf, winning or losing has never been a big deal as far as I was concerned, a few pounds changing hands here and there was of no matter when put into the context of the overall picture. Having the means both time wise and financially was all important – albeit that I was rather late in life starting this new hobby when 48 years of age but it was all made very worthwhile by the wide range of the

My sister Glad and her husband with great grandson Josh, 1992.

Two of my golfing friends of many years standing.

new friends made from all walks of life and backgrounds. How did I come to be playing regularly with a serving Major General? (I must admit to advising him of my ex-military status 'Corporal' which evoked considerable amusement! Mere Colonels, Majors, Captains then paled into insignificance!) Especially as another regular colleague was a retired chippy (carpenter).

At one time when I was a member of Long Ashton Golf Club, Bristol, I found myself playing regularly with show business people appearing at the Bristol Hippodrome, never failing to be amazed at their ignorance with regards to what went on in the world outside their show-biz sphere! Characters were always to be found, some with whom one preferred not to become too deeply involved, others a delight to call friends. One such at Broadstone was Ben, a dour forthright character who was never slow to call a spade a spade – and that's putting it mildly! Many of his tales (mostly concerning lady friends!) during his spell as a DR (dispatch rider) in UK and Italy during the war were too far fetched to be other than true – unfortunately only a few can be re-counted here! Such as, when attending a village dance and slipping out to attend to the needs of a young lady in the darkness behind the village hall he found himself being used as a urinal by an unsuspecting squaddie who must have been completely startled with Ben's advice proferred in no uncertain terms!

On another occasion when waiting to start playing, the three of us were approached by a fourth person who asked if he could join us. 'No,' said Ben, 'because I don't ******* **** like you!' and on a similar occasion 'No, because you cheat!'

Ben was self appointed 'Spoof' champion of Dorset! I must admit he won more frequently than most. Playing on one occasion with someone who had been a golfing friend of his for over 20 years, Ben saw him drop a match (each person had 3 matches or coins) and when he claimed the win Ben went mad. 'You deliberately dropped a match,' threw him out of the school and never played golf or spoof with him again. Playing a fourball in front of an army Colonel and his wife, they drove into us on a short hole and were duly taken to task by Ben – in typical army language, 'the only sort he knows'. On arrival at the clubhouse we were met by a very embarrassed secretary who had been advised as to the happenings at the short hole, our explanation and apologies were accepted, none were offered by Ben!

I particularly liked the story told by Ben of an occasion when playing in a fourball on a very open course in Norfolk. They were following a ladies' match and one of Ben's group had a pressing need to spend a penny but no trees in sight! With the ladies' match on a short hole in front the gentleman could wait no longer and turning his back on the ladies, duly relieved himself. He arrived at the clubhouse to be told by the secretary that the lady captain (one of ladies' match) had reported him and he would have to appear before the committee at the next meeting. Duly appearing and told of the complaint he said, 'She is quite right and I plead guilty, my only defence is that whilst she could see what I was doing, she couldn't see what I was doing it with! It was a very cold day and I could only just see it and I was holding it!' The meeting dissolved in laughter! I must admit to sharing a great affinity with Ben, apart from his dalliances with numerous lady friends all of those I met held him in great affection.

Ben had a softer side as evidenced by the fact that when I was lying helpless in harness for some 5–6 weeks following my accident he turned up every day during mealtimes and spoon fed me with various soups and sweets which I was unable to do myself. Entirely without prompting he went to Blandford and took dozens of photographs of the new building work to enable me to keep up to date with progress – something I really appreciated. Following my recovery and the operation to insert a steel plate in my neck (to hold my head on – I was told) Ben was the first to encourage me to walk and then take up playing again with them, despite my total inability to perform to anything like my previous standard. I was very sad when Ben, fully aware I think of the onset of Parkinsons Disease, decided to resign his membership. I cannot believe that the fact he could no longer perform to his previous level would have influenced this. Ben, who had spent a very adventurous life as a rally driver, motor cycle cross champion and army skier was not one to throw in the towel without a fight!

Inevitably my original circle of golfing friends have almost all passed on: Ben, David, a previous scratch golfer who lost a leg to gangrene, Charlie, a very low handicap golfer and first class teacher of the game, and ex RAF pilot; ex-publican Jack, Cyril another ex-publican and Vic who dabbled in all sorts – not all entirely above board! Vic had a very undulating garden and as he was by no means an enthusiastic gardener, he adorned his lawn with numerous gnomes. Waking one morning to a bare lawn he phoned the police who duly rang back minutes later to tell Vic his gnomes were queued at a local bus stop and would he please arrange to pick them up! This story particularly amused author Leslie Thomas, a frequent member of our golfing group.

Disaster occurred in late 1990. I had arranged to spend a week golfing at St. Mellion, taking a friend with me, others to follow the next day. I was driving along the Bridport by-pass less than a mile from where I lived before the war, with no others cars in front or behind me. There were a lot of cars

approaching me, some 20–30 off, two abreast as allowed by the
road markings, when the first in line approaching me was
shunted from behind and, completely without warning,
directly into my path about 10–12 ft away. I was travelling at
about 55–60 mph and later learnt that the other car was doing
about 40–45mph. Therefore a collision was inevitable,
impossible for either of us to take any action at all. I was
driving a Mercedes, which struck the Volkswagen side on,
crushing it out of all recognition. I was told later my car flew
at least 30 yards through the air finishing up facing the
opposite direction. Both occupants of the VW were killed
outright. When I recovered consciousness, having been saved
by my seat belt and the fact that I was driving a strongly built
car, I was in great pain and unable to move. I was eventually
removed and taken to Weymouth hospital where it was found
I had broken my neck in two places. Unfortunately, my
colleague suffered even worse injuries, it took half an hour for
him to be released from the car, and he later found he had
suffered horrendous chest and rib injuries, spending 6 weeks in
intensive care and never recovering anything approaching his
original fitness. Even now, over 10 years later, he is unable to
walk without a stick. Once again there was a tragic
coincidence, after 2 days at Weymouth hospital I was moved
to Poole hospital and put under an Orthopaedic Consultant
who was shortly moving on from that post. The doctor who
had died in the accident was on his way back from a holiday in
Cornwall prior to taking up the orthopaedic consultant's job at
Poole hospital! A driver was subsequently convicted of
dangerous driving and at the inquest it was stated that neither
driver had time to take any evasive action prior to the
collision, although this did little to lessen my feelings of guilt.
This feeling was not improved when I received a very

unpleasant letter from the deceased doctor's mother, which I felt sure had been written when under great sense of loss and distress. I burnt it straight away before anyone else had a chance to read it, not even telling my wife.

After 6 weeks in intensive treatment in hospital I was discharged, pending a major operation to have a steel plate inserted in my neck, this being the only way in which I could be relieved of the persistent pain, frequent spells of paralysis and the always present pins and needles. These are still very much in evidence, but not noticed as time and familiarity has led to me ignoring such feelings. Hospitals in the UK had been put on standby at that time, due to the Suez Canal crisis, and it was not until June 1991, 6 months later, that I was admitted to the spinal unit at Southampton Hospital where a very successful operation was performed to cut away the bones pressing on the spinal cord and insert a plate to hold my head on.

A further tragic turn of events saw my wife of 52 years die suddenly whilst I was waiting to go into hospital, and the very same day my son Michael's boy, 18 year old Stuart, was involved in a very serious road accident, this within 20 hours of my wife's death. Being such serious news it was kept from me for a further 24 hours. Fortunately, Stuart is very strong both physically and mentally and has recovered completely and with his two brothers is now working in the business.

Just prior to my accident, work had started on a large extension to the works and with Brian and Mike now fully in charge and running the whole shooting match. This extension, including new offices, was all completed and in operation when I was eventually able to return to work (after leaving for a 7 day golfing holiday some 9 months before!). For some months after my return, lack of neck/head movement made it very difficult for me to pick up on office work again, particularly coping with that part involving computers. Before the accident I had checked and entered all incoming orders on the computer, plus releasing/printing delivery notes/instructions, but found this very stressful, eventually having the keyboard and VDU removed from my desk so that I should not be tempted into doing this type of work. I therefore concentrated on re-arranging the layout of the factory to take the best advantage of the extra space now available, which has proved to be very successful.

We always endeavoured, when contemplating purchases of new plant and processes, to invest in the very latest equipment and this has paid off handsomely. We were the first company in the UK to install an innovative French upstroke press brake, buying the demonstration machine directly off the stand at a London exhibition. Part of the terms agreed were that we should allow other interested UK companies to visit our works and see a demonstration of the machine in use, which offer was taken up by over 20 firms! We also installed the very first (in the west of England) paint spraying, dry epoxy resin powder coating equipment.

From the outset when designing new items for hospitals, we followed simple guidelines: ensuring that the items would do the job intended in a way most acceptable to the user; also that the design was as straightforward and uncomplicated as possible, requiring absolute minimal maintenance, if any, with the price being the last consideration. This latter factor probably worked against us in the short term, but we are satisfied that it is the right approach in the long term.

Some 40 plus years ago, we made an application for a patent for a system of adjustable self-supporting shelves in medicine cupboards. After spending over £200 (a fortune in those days) obtaining a provisional patent, when applying for a full patent 12 months later, it was refused on the grounds that this was a copy of a provisional patent taken out in New Zealand in 1906! Drawings of this item were enclosed illustrating a wire mesh item designed to hold flower pots on the wall!

This bore no relation whatsoever to our application, but it would have cost a fortune to contest. We did learn, however, that our application meant that once registered no one else could produce this item for at least a year, and it certainly could not be patented by ourselves or others in the future. Since that time we have made several applications, always with the object of preventing it being copied, never proceeding beyond the patent applied for stage.

There have been numerous cases where our designs have been copied, but we have found that in the long term ours has prevailed, to the extent that whilst we are still progressing favourably, almost without exception those who copied our designs are no longer in existence, possibly inevitable, as it must show a basic lack of business acumen.

There have been several instances where Ministry of Health departments have taken part in such debatable exercises. Some 20 years after we first introduced our medicine trolley we were asked to forward a sample to their Elephant & Castle offices for evaluation. This we did, only to be asked a couple of months later to collect same. Making enquiries when doing this I was told that numerous firms across the country had been shown our trolley and asked to submit design and prices for a similar trolley, but not ourselves! Nothing ever came of their efforts however, and we are still the only firm making this type of trolley in any quantity.

Some 25 years ago when central supply units were being formed across the country, using pre-packed sets of sterilised instruments, dressings and syringes etc., we realised that the then conventional type of instrument trolley was not entirely suitable, having a flat stainless steel top and shelf held in position by corner tubes extending above the level of the top, and thus not allowing the outer wrapping of the sterile packs to be easily opened. Also, of course, the flat surface of the top allowed round items to roll off when the trolley was moved.

We could easily have made shelves with 3 upturned flanges to overcome both these problems – but at a price. Only imperial size sheet (6ft x 3ft or 8ft x 4ft) was readily available within the UK. Whereas a single 6ft x 3ft sheet could be cut to make 8 shelves for 18" x 18" trolleys, with flanged shelves only 3 off could be made from the same size sheet. Having had an enquiry from a new London Hospital for a large number of trolleys with the flanged shelves, we designed a trolley offering the same size fixed top, with upturned flanges, with flanged shelf to slightly smaller dimensions, this also enabling 8 shelves for 18" x 18" trolley to be cut from same sheet as before.

I took this prototype trolley, together with a standard trolley, to the hospital concerned, who showed great interest and asked me to leave both for their evaluation. 2 weeks later we were asked to collect the standard trolley, leaving the prototype for further evaluation.

Some 5 weeks later we received a curt telephone call saying this had been finalised and the trolley could be collected. I chose to collect it myself, and on arrival a very junior clerk was told to fetch the trolley for me. When taking it to my car I asked him how the trolley had been received, being taken aback to be advised, somewhat enthusiastically, that it had been widely acclaimed by the 6 firms invited to inspect it and asked to quote, and that an order had been placed with one of them. We were not even asked to do other than the first invitation to quote for the standard trolley, and a year or so later our prototype design found itself the subject of a British Standard!

There was nothing much that we could do about it, although I did write a letter asking if the design was found to be satisfactory, and despite sending a further letter requesting an answer, no reply was ever received.

Many years previously we had been asked to submit a sample of a large pedal bin to a Northern hospital, subsequently being asked to collect it a few weeks later without ever being asked to quote, only to find on a subsequent visit some 12 months later that they were very much in evidence. Again overt questioning of junior staff elicited information that all these new bins had been made by a local firm. We have always been aware that it is very easy for an unscrupulous supplies officer to obtain considerably lower quotes for most items if the quoting firm is provided with something to copy, no design, advertising and allied expenses incurred. The only problem is that if the user wants a repeat order for a small quantity at a later date there is very little chance of them being able to obtain it from the same source. Which is something that another hospital found to its cost when a quantity of medicine cupboards (all made as our sample) were bought elsewhere, then found it impossible to get repeat supplies, or even replacement locks and keys in the same mastered suite when they were next required.

Count Down – the Vanishing Years

When I first started in business, apart from my desire to 'have a go' and see if I had what it takes my object was to achieve the best possible living standards for my family.

Once firmly established the aim was to build something which could be passed onto my sons and grandchildren. I have never had the urge to change my lifestyle for the high life – family and golf are preferred to boating or world travel. I loved the challenge of finding solutions to problems put to us by hospitals across the UK and couldn't get in early enough in the morning to see what the day's mail produced. I even took to collecting the mail from the post office sorting room rather than wait for the 8.30a.m. delivery. Of late, I was becoming more and more concerned as to the direction being taken by the company. From the outset I had made a great point of welcoming all enquiries – whether in our field or otherwise, responding by return, advising not in our area or requesting further details and visit by our representative if preferred – with the thought always in the background that if we could provide an answer to that particular hospital's problem, surely it would also serve for other hospitals.

Over the years we built up a reputation for problem solving and have been told many times the enquirer rang us as they had been advised to do so by another hospital where we had solved their problem. It is a fact that probably in excess of 90% of enquires received at our sales desks are prefaced 'Do you make' or 'Can you help me'.

I was therefore appalled to find that our reps had been told not to encourage enquiries unless for something already shown in our catalogue and immediately countermanded this instruction. After all, apart from a few 'British Standard' or similar items, everything shown in our catalogue resulted from such a request 'can you/do you make?' I am adamant that the long term future of a small company such as ours depends on the production of new designs made specifically to meet the hospitals' requirements and not to restrict ourselves to offering only that which we want to sell.

I continued transferring shares equally to my sons, eventually arriving at the position when my wife and myself held a 52% stake in the company.

Over the first 20–25 years we received numerous approaches from both UK and overseas concerns as to whether we would consider outright or partial disposal of the company, replying to all that we were a family owned and managed company and had no intention of ever considering such approaches. In several instances we received replies complimenting us on our attitude.

My wife had many times expressed concern as to the future of the company once I was no longer involved, my sons having totally different personalities and interests in life outside of work. My answer always was that this is something which I could not legislate for and could only try and achieve by long term aim of equality to both sons. When ultimately I did return to work after my accident, I was unable to pick up where I had left off and really regarded work as a therapy with my taking a back seat due to the very much reduced standards of which I was now capable.

I shall be forever grateful to my sons, and in more recent years to my grandsons, for their wholehearted support, always given regardless of time, effort and inconvenience involved – even if not always entirely in agreement with me. Without such commitment the company could not possibly have reached its present status.

This equally applies to our staff whom I have always endeavoured to involve in developing proposed new designs, welcoming their input. Who better to advise than the person expected to carry out such work with their knowledge of what was possible with the available plant, allied to their expertise when they could frequently suggest alternative ways, possibly enabling short cuts to be taken to reduce manufacturing time and achieve required end product.

The inevitable split at work eventually arrived, both Brian and myself were rarely consulted over company policy and day to day running and when we were it was almost always in retrospect such action already having been already taken. From Michael's point of view this was quite normal as he had been virtually running the company. Brian, not being very interested in the day to day largely computerised work involved, was very much a hands on type – as was his son Russell. Brian therefore decided to retire, with the company buying back his shares. Largely out of loyalty to his father, Russell also decided to opt out and the company also bought his shares. My action in retaining controlling interest of 52% really backfired when my wife died and the Inland Revenue therefore placed a much higher valuation on our shares, lumped together with death duty assessment, resulting in a huge tax bill, albeit spread over 10 years. Subsequently I transferred all shares equally to my sons.

The biggest sorrow of my life is that neither of my parents lived to share in what success has been achieved, and not being able to repay them for the many sacrifices they must have made for us children, and for bringing us up to show and have respect for others, whether due or not. Also that Glad was taken so quickly from us before being able to see her great grandsons, Joshua and Thomas, whom she would have spoiled even more than our sons and their families, all of whom meant the world to her and represented the consuming interest in her life – apart from her love of tea – indulged in at every opportunity day or night. On one occasion after spending a week on holiday at a very posh hotel in Lausanne (where there was a porter on every floor 24 hours a day), shortly after returning home we received a supplementary bill for over £100 in respect of tea supplied. This was nearly 30 years ago when the bill for 5 of us for the weeks' accommodation was less the £500!

Glad loved her home and family and never looked forward to going on holiday, as evidenced by the fact that within 48 hours of arrival at a hotel, she began packing up ready to return home! Come Thursday, 'Shall we go home tomorrow?' this despite numerous phone calls to ensure everything all right with sons, wives and families!

Returning to the work theme:

Reminiscing, I recall a couple of events which possibly taught us a lot about people, and employees in particular. We were very pleased that a youngster who joined us straight from school showed particular promise as a sheet metal worker. He was duly rewarded with pay rises far above the norm and we were delighted when he told us he wanted to learn to drive, so that he could get a car. I actually took him for a few runs in my car and found he was a natural. He bought a car, although he couldn't drive without a qualified driver, of course, but soon found fellow employees willing to take him out. Eventually he told me he had put in for his test and could he and one of our staff have a couple of hours off to take his test? I agreed, telling him and his pal not to bother to clock out, and wishing him success.

He returned very crestfallen to say he had failed, I took him for another drive and was impressed enough to encourage him to apply for another test as soon as he could. He did, and went with the same pal and came back highly chuffed. He came straight up to me, I congratulated him, and was more than slightly taken aback when he asked if he could have his cards on Friday and leave without working any notice? He then revealed that he had been offered a job driving a dumper at almost twice his current rate of pay with a firm building a local by-pass!

So much for loyalty, at least when he left I didn't offer him any holiday pay and he was not brass necked enough to ask for it. There must be a moral in that story somewhere!

In a totally different vein, a very keen 15 year old expressed interest in brazing, then oxyacetylene welding and graduated to argon arc stainless steel welding. The latter, by far the hardest technique, he really relished and was very quickly excelling men 20 years his senior both in quality of work and speed. We repaid him to the extent that when aged 17 he was on the same rate as his elders. One day I had a visit from his father who asked how he was progressing, expressed his delight, then said did we provide papers to confirm same, to which I responded who wanted papers when he could show his ability on the bench. His father insisted that he should have certificates and to satisfy him, not his son, we arranged a 12 month 2 days a week release course with British Oxygen Company at a local college.

He duly obtained his papers, but on return to full time work we soon found he had become so bogged down with theory that he had lost all his previous natural ability. Within a few months we had to take him off welding and he soon left us. We lost touch with him, but always wondered if he had used his papers to get employment elsewhere as a stainless steel welder, and to what end!

One rather amusing, although really pathetic, case was again that of a 16 year old who showed great potential as a sheet metal worker when fed all the information needed to produce an item, initial size of sheet metal required, cropping and bending details etc. I instructed the foreman to give him a job where he could work out all the dimensions on his own. After an hour or so he presented the foreman with a sheet showing all the correct dimensions – including bending and forming allowances, but showing these something like; $17"$ + $\frac{1}{2}"$ + $\frac{1}{8}"$ + half a $\frac{1}{16}"$ with the next dimension similarly detailed. His schooling had never progressed to the stage where he could ever express it as, say $20\frac{7}{32}" \times 16\frac{9}{16}"$. However, he went on to become a very useful employee! Possibly he would have done better in these days of metrification.

I learnt many lessons myself when attending exhibitions, observing how so-called experienced sales staff on other stands behaved. Apart from skiving off at every possible opportunity, and spending more time talking to staff on other stands and arranging their evening junketing (at their firm's expense) than to the visitors to their stand, shoving a folder and a few leaflets into their hands and leaving them to get on with it! One actually told me once that he was surprised to see me waste so much time talking to four student nurses who were only, in his words, 'collecting catalogues to show their superiors they had visited the exhibition'. He was quite taken aback when I asked him where he thought the sisters (and matrons) of the future were going to come from? And had he thought that in a few years time he might well be wanting to make appointments to meet these student nurses. In fact I found out for myself on many a later occasion, that even if you didn't remember them – they certainly *did* remember you!

In retrospect – would/should I have done things differently?

Most definitely yes – particularly as I always adhered to the rule that 'If you can't pay for it – you can't afford it,' broken only when short term HP was employed to enable purchase of highly desirable piece of plant. This is no longer applicable regarding finance today, far removed from the days when your local bank manager frowned on every proposed expenditure and frequently made you think again and call it a day!

I was never one to sit on the fence (pig headed comes to mind!) always regarding any action as a step forward, even if you slipped back half a pace at least you were still further on than before, always providing that one took on board the reason for the half pace slip and did not repeat it.

This learning curve, 'profit from your mistakes', is one I have tried to apply in all areas – particularly when designing something radically new, being a great believer in the saying, 'If you haven't made a mistake – you haven't made anything.'

Over the years I have repeatedly been asked by friends when I was going to pack it all in and retire, my response always being that I regarded work as an enjoyable therapy and when I ceased to enjoy it, I would call it a day.

Regrettably that day has now arrived. I simply do not enjoy going to work and have therefore scaled down my involvement to a few hours a day – and even that not every day. I hope that son and grandsons have regard to my almost 50 years of knowledge, but regret this is rarely requested and when proffered rarely acted upon.

In conclusion – I must pay tribute to the two Glads in my life.

My wife was a wonderful mother as both our sons and daughters-in-law will confirm. As will Russell's dog, Tiger, who always looked forward to our visits and his sandwich treats.

Always ready to receive confidencies and help out in any way possible, morally, financially or merely sympathy, Glad had the knack of seeing through people and one was never left in doubt as to her view. I remember her total refusal to learn to drive (she did try!) and also to fly (which she never did!) But she was fully prepared to accept the family decision – even though this meant camping out in the foulest of weather!

Sister Glad was a real soulmate until we left school, but even then sharing confidencies, a great friend to my wife, particularly when I was away during the war, and later having Brian for several weeks every summer – something he always remembers. She was a great pillar of the church – always prepared to do more than her fair share of work both in the church and helping sick/infirm parishioners in their homes.

When her son's marriage broke up, without hesitation, she took his two young daughters into her home for many years until they were old enough to go their own ways. Both have repeatedly told me how grateful they were and how devastated when she died.

I could wish for no greater epitaph than to be compared in some small measure to both Glads!